MASTERING THE CHAIN: A COMPREHENSIVE GUIDE TO ELEVATING EFFICIENCY THROUGH STRATEGIC INVENTORY MANAGEMENT

Subharun Pal

© Subharun Pal 2023

All rights reserved by the author. No part of this publication may be reproduced, stored in a retrieval system, or transmitted in any form or by any means, electronic, mechanical, photocopying, recording, or otherwise, without the prior permission of the author.

Although every precaution has been taken to verify the accuracy of the information contained herein, the author and publisher assume no responsibility for any errors or omissions. No liability is assumed for damages that may result from the use of the information contained within.

Title: Mastering the Chain: A Comprehensive Guide to Elevating Efficiency through Strategic Inventory Management
Language: English
Character set encoding: UTF-8

First published by

An Imprint of BlueRose Publishers

Head Office: B-6, 2nd Floor,
ABL Workspaces, Block B, Sector 4,
Noida, Uttar Pradesh 201301
M: +91-8882 898 898

This tome is assiduously consecrated to those often overlooked yet indubitably pivotal cogs in the labyrinthine apparatus of commercial enterprise: the logisticians and inventory custodians of supply chain management. You stand as the veritable savants of operational efficacy, the maestros of systemic harmonisation, and the intrepid cartographers charting the Byzantine topography of logistical deployment. Through your scrupulous strategizing, prescient foresight, and indefatigable exertions, you ensure the expeditious materialisation of merchandise in its designated locus at the opportune juncture, thereby transmuting the quotidian transactions of purchase and sale into a near-mystical tableau of fluidity.

Whilst your labours might elude the perceptive faculties of the casual consumer, who unreflectively saunters into a retail establishment or cursorily actuates a digital interface, it is inarguable that without your infrastructural scaffolding, the spectrum of consumer choices would precipitously contract, if not vanish in toto. The magnitudinal impact you exert upon consumer gratification and entrepreneurial triumph, though predominantly sub rosa, is ineffaceable. This manuscript stands as an encomium to your indispensable accoutrements, a veneration of your unparalleled acumen, and a pedagogical compendium to facilitate your continued journey towards professional apotheosis.

I further extend this dedication unto my sagacious mentors and pedagogues, those who have significantly augmented my apprehension of mercantile logistics and incited me to probe into the sinuous intricacies of supply chain governance. Your erudition and perspicacious counsel have served as my celestial Polaris, guiding me through the manifold subtleties and abstruse complexities that render this discipline so inexhaustibly compelling and quintessential.

To my professional confederates and intellectual coevals, my gratitude is effusive for serving as the resonant chamber against which I have tested my conjectures and postulations. Our dialectical engagements have imparted dimensionality and amplitude to this literary endeavour. Your quotidian devotion to boundary-pushing praxis within our occupational sphere stands as a perpetual wellspring of inspiration.

To my familial consortium, your unwavering moral buttress has functioned as my foundational bedrock. The myriad hours apportioned away from your presence during the authorial gestation of this volume were mitigated by your compassionate comprehension and affective solidarity. I am encumbered with a substantial pecuniary and emotional indebtedness to each of you for your steadfast companionship during this monumental enterprise.

In summation, to all commercial entities, whether titanic conglomerates or fledgling ventures, earnestly endeavouring to adapt, innovate, and flourish in an increasingly convoluted and competitive marketplace: may this tome serve as your lighthouse, illuminating the path towards unparalleled operational dexterity and unprecedented commercial triumph.

With consummate gratitude and unalloyed veneration,

- **Subharun Pal**

ACKNOWLEDGEMENTS

The odyssey towards the fruition of "**Mastering the Chain: A Comprehensive Guide to Elevating Efficiency through Strategic Inventory Management**" has been a diurnally exigent yet ineffably fulfilling expedition. Though marked by interminable epochs of empirical inquiry, assiduous composition, and iterative refinement, this magnum opus would have been an unattainable chimera absent the unwavering benison of a consortium of sagacious and altruistic individuals. Ergo, it is imperative to apportion a momentary interlude to tender due encomium to the invaluable collaborators whose contributions metamorphosed this literary aspirant into a tangible exegesis.

In primis, an effusive ovation is in order for the venerable savants, academic illuminati, and professional compatriots who magnanimously disseminated their specialised perspicacity and dexterity. The calibre and cogency of your contributions have been instrumental in sculpting the thematic architecture of this tome whilst buttressing its empirical veracity and contextual pertinence. Equally, my appreciative sentiments are extended to the editorial and typographical syndicate whose punctilious scrutiny, incisive sapience, and unwavering commitment to qualitative apotheosis transmuted an embryonic manuscript into a lustrous, publication-ready scholarly artefact.

To my ineffable consort, Sharmistha, your amorevole solicitude and fiduciary support have served as my metaphysical Pharos throughout this onerous literary sojourn. The nocturnal vigils, the hebdomadal marathons of authorial exertion, and the expansive litter of inchoate drafts strewn across our domestic banqueting table—these you have elegantly negotiated with an indefatigable élan and a ceaseless infusion of caffeinated elixirs. You are the axiomatic fulcrum upon which my existential equilibrium teeters, and the actualisation of this book would have been illusory sans your foundational anchorage.

To my progenitors, Malin Chandra Pal and Bina Pal, lexical eloquence falters in articulating the depth of my indebtedness for your lifelong endowment of nurturance and galvanisation. The axiological constructs of industriousness and tenacity that you have inculcated within me have been meticulously transposed into this endeavour and reverberate across the tapestry of my quotidian existence. This manuscript stands as a eulogistic monument to the nurturing pedagogy and unconditional amore you dispensed from my incipient sentience.

A distinct commendation is reserved for our diminutive scion, Ayansh, whose nascent biennial existence infuses quotidian ebullience even subsequent to the most Herculean literary undertakings. Your untrammelled inquisitiveness and inexhaustible vigour function as daily clarion calls to the multiplicity of life's quotidian miracles. While your tender cognition may not yet fathom the exactitude of your paternal figure's literary preoccupations, your mere corporeal ubiquity suffuses copious stimuli for inspiration.

In ultimate analysis, an unfeigned obeisance to you, the erudite interlocutor. By consecrating your temporal resources to this intellectual corpus, you validate the momentousness of its subject matter and assimilate into an intellectual cadaver in quest of preeminent efficacy and optimisation within the purview of inventory stewardship. It is my sanguine aspiration that the didactic repository encapsulated herein facilitates your assiduous journey towards chain mastery.

With unbounded gratitude and utmost deference,

Subharun Pal

PREFACE

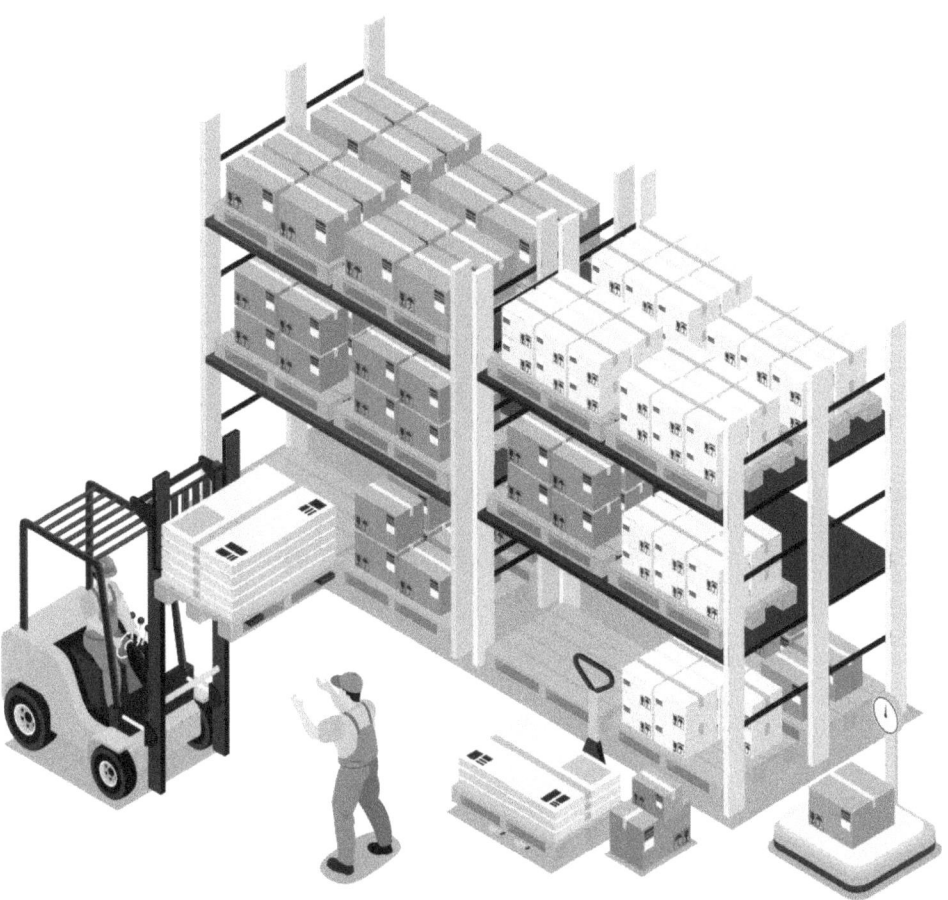

Welcome to "**Mastering the Chain: A Comprehensive Guide to Elevating Efficiency through Strategic Inventory Management**," a book designed to serve as a definitive resource for professionals, scholars, and students in the ever-evolving landscape of supply chain management. If you're reading this, you likely understand that inventory management is not a mere storage task, but a strategic activity interwoven with forecasting, data analysis, and supply chain collaboration.

In the following chapters, you will encounter a holistic overview of inventory management—from foundational theories and models to cutting-edge innovations and empirical analyses. This book aims to bridge the gap between academic rigor and practical application, demystifying complex methodologies and models while highlighting their relevance in real-world scenarios.

Who Should Read This Book?

Whether you're an operations manager in charge of a complex supply chain, a scholar seeking the latest research and trends, or a student looking to grasp the fundamentals of inventory management, this book offers valuable insights. It's also designed for consultants, strategists, and executives aiming to optimize their organisation's supply chain efficacy.

How to Navigate This Book

The book is structured to provide a seamless journey through the intricate world of inventory management:

- **Chapter 1** sets the stage by introducing the fundamentals of supply chain optimisation.
- **Chapter 2** dives deep into inventory types, costs, and trade-offs, offering a conceptual foundation.
- **Chapter 3** and **4** tackle forecasting and optimization models, respectively, tools vital for effective inventory management.
- **Chapters 5** and **6** focus on technological advances in inventory visibility and tracking, as well as the critical aspect of inventory accuracy.
- **Chapter 7** discusses the growing importance of supply chain collaboration and vendor-managed inventory in an increasingly interconnected and volatile marketplace.
- **Chapter 8** specifically addresses the challenges and strategies involved in managing inventory in e-commerce and omni-channel retailing, the fields undergoing rapid changes in the digital era.
- **Chapter 9** covers the performance metrics and KPIs necessary to evaluate the efficiency of your inventory management strategy.
- **Chapter 10** delves into the implementation of supply chain optimization strategies, giving actionable insights for practitioners.
- **Chapter 11** provides empirical analyses through real-world case studies to validate the strategies and frameworks discussed.
- Finally, **Chapter 12** gazes into the future, outlining innovative technologies and trends that are reshaping the

supply chain landscape.

A Journey Towards Efficiency

It's a transformative period for the world of inventory management and supply chains at large. Technological advances, consumer expectations, and global dynamics are continuously altering the landscape. "**Mastering the Chain**" is designed to be your compass in navigating these complexities, offering actionable insights, robust models, and a vision for the future.

As you embark on this journey, may you find this book not just an academic discourse but a toolkit—one that helps you elevate efficiency, optimize resource utilisation, and unlock new opportunities in the realm of inventory management.

Here's to mastering the chain!

Sincerely,

Subharun Pal

Now, let the journey begin.

PROLOGUE

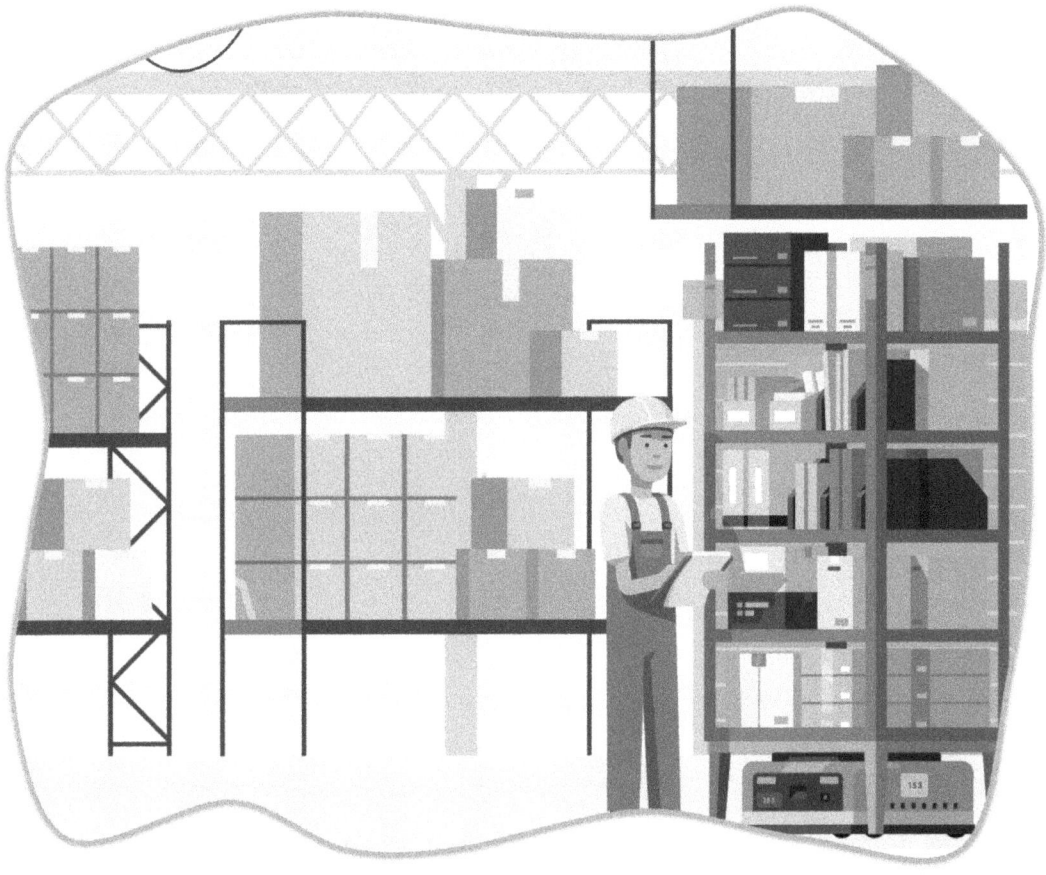

In the grand tapestry of business, every function has its own distinct artistry, from marketing's compelling narratives to finance's numerical finesse. However, inventory management—often viewed as the less glamorous cousin of these functions—holds a transformative power that is both under-appreciated and underestimated.

You may consider inventory as mere 'stock,' an afterthought relegated to dusty warehouses. Yet, it's so much more: it is the lifeblood coursing through the veins of a business, affecting everything from cash flow to customer satisfaction. Mastering this vital element can exponentially elevate your business operations, infusing them with efficiency, profitability, and sustainability.

"**Mastering the Chain: A Comprehensive Guide to Elevating Efficiency through Strategic Inventory Management**" aims to be your definitive handbook in understanding this essential but often neglected aspect of business. We'll delve into how inventory management is not just an operational chore but a strategic necessity, its mastery central to a well-orchestrated business model.

Beyond the jargon of SKUs, JIT, FIFO, and LIFO, this book aims to equip you with practical insights, real-world examples, and actionable strategies. Whether you're a budding entrepreneur, an inventory manager, or a seasoned business executive, the goal is to elevate your understanding of inventory management from a mere logistical function to a strategic tool capable of delivering significant business advantages.

In a fast-paced world replete with unpredictability, those who can most effectively control their supply chain are those who will stand ahead of the competition. Whether it's responding to a global pandemic, a bottleneck in global shipping, or even just the seasonal ebb and flow of consumer demand, mastering your inventory chain provides a buffer against uncertainty.

By the end of this book, inventory management will no longer be a 'box to check off' but a transformative approach that enhances every facet of your business, from procurement to production to profit. Welcome to the journey of Mastering the Chain.

Prepare to unlock the untapped potential that lies in the hidden corners of your warehouses and the complex matrices of your spreadsheets, elevating your business strategy to new heights of efficiency and effectiveness.

Let's get started.

POETIC BLURB

In the labyrinth of ledgers and logistics, where boxes and bytes dance in a delicate ballet, lies a hidden alchemy: the science of supply, the art of inventory. "**Mastering the Chain**" is more than a guide; it's a revelation. With eloquence it unveils the secret symphony that turns chaos into cadence, elevating efficiency from mere metric to mindful mastery. Here, strategy weds substance, and wisdom wears the robe of real-world application. Unlock the intricacies of inventory management with this comprehensive tome and let your business become an orchestrated opus of optimised operations. A must-read for those who seek the sublime in the systematic.

In the labyrinthine waltz of ledger and lore,
Where box meets byte in a mythical score,
Rests a hidden alchemy of infinite grace—
The choreography of supply, inventory's embrace.

"Mastering the Chain," a scripture divine,
Reveals the arcane symphony that intertwines.
Chaos turned cadence, mayhem morphed to muse,
An elegant manifesto the artful can use.

From the inner sanctums of warehouse gloom
To the bustling stage of the retail room—
Find strategies woven with wisdom's thread,
And paths where pioneering footsteps tread.

Unlock the sacred scrolls of efficiency's hymn,
Where strategy ascends, no longer a whim.
Wisdom cloaked in practicality's glance,
Invites you now, to take your chance.

Within these pages—ripe for keen eyes—
Lies a chain's mastery, devoid of disguise.
Embark, dear reader, your quest in view,
To make your own opus, forever anew.

ABOUT THE AUTHOR

Subharun Pal, an exemplar of scholastic perspicuity and methodological rigor, is simultaneously immersed in an advanced program of academic inquiry within the prestigious corridors of the Swiss School of Management (SSM) in Switzerland and the eminent European International University (EIU) in France. His intellectual fiefdom traverses an interdisciplinary confluence of computer science engineering, pioneering disruptive technological paradigms, tactical operations management, holistic logistics integratives, comprehensive supply chain orchestration, intricate fiscal analytics, complex commercial jurisprudential frameworks, and educational epistemology.

Further buttressing his academic portfolio are nuanced engagements with premier pedagogical establishments, such as IIT Jammu, IIT Patna, IIM Calcutta, IIM Ranchi, Edith Cowan University Perth, CII-Institute of Logistics Chennai, National University of Juridical Sciences Kolkata, Karnataka State Open University Mysore, and Visvesvaraya Technological University Belgaum. His scholarly cachet is redoubled by accolades and endorsements from global organisational entities including The World Bank, KPMG, Cisco, Microsoft, Oracle, EC Council, Exemplar Global Inc., ISEL Global Canada, APMG UK, ISI Bangalore, NIIT, ILI New Delhi, SHRI Singapore, and TüV Süd Akademie.

Epitomising the apogee of intellectual acumen, Pal's unflagging pursuit of academic excellence has manifested in an expansive corpus of incisive research monographs, erudite exegetical treatises, and groundbreaking patents, all of which bear both transcontinental and intra-national pertinence. In addition to these scholastic accomplishments, his substantive governance in editorial oversight and participation in scholarly colloquia reinforce his indomitable commitment to the intellectual proliferation and enhancement of multifarious academic disciplines. Such concerted endeavours have not only solidified his distinction within the international scholarly ecosystem but have also garnered him an array of laudatory commendations, thus accentuating his dominant eminence within the global intelligentsia.

CONTENTS

Copyright Declaration	II
Dedication	V
Acknowledgements	VII
Preface	IX
Prologue	XIII
Poetic Blurb	XVI
About the Author	XVIII

Chapter 1

Chapter 1: Introduction to Supply Chain Optimisation	27
Understanding the Fundamental Imperatives of Supply Chain Optimisation	27
Key Concepts and Definitions: A Deep Dive	28
Benefits of Efficient Inventory Management within the Supply Chain Framework	29

Chapter 2

Chapter 2: Fundamentals of Inventory Management	31
The Pivotal Role of Inventory in Supply Chain Dynamics	31
Types of Inventories in Strategic Supply Chain Management	32
Inventory Costs and Trade-offs: Navigating the Economic Landscape of Supply Chain Management	33
Trade-offs in Inventory Management	33
Inventory Control Techniques: A Scholarly Dive into Operational Efficacy	34

Chapter 3

Chapter 3: Forecasting and Demand Planning	37
The Imperative of Precise Demand Forecasting in Modern Inventory Management	37
Techniques for Demand Forecasting	38
Collaborative Demand Planning	39
Demand Variability and Safety Stock	40

Chapter 4

Chapter 4: Inventory Optimization Models	41
Economic Order Quantity (EOQ) Model: A Critical Analysis	41
Reorder Point (ROP) Model: A Quantitative Framework for Strategic Inventory Optimisation	42
Just-in-Time (JIT) Inventory Management: A Multifaceted Paradigm for Operational Efficiency and Strategic Excellence	43
ABC Analysis and Pareto Principle: Cornerstones of Strategic Inventory Management in the Supply Chain Landscape	45

Chapter 5

Utilizing Technology for Real-time Inventory Visibility: A Critical Discourse   47

Barcode and RFID Technology: Pioneering Efficiency in Inventory Management   48

Warehouse Management Systems (WMS): A Locus of Technological Transformation in Modern Inventory Management Paradigms   49

Optimal Inventory Tracking Protocols in Contemporary Business Environments   49

Chapter 6
Chapter 6: Inventory Accuracy and Cycle Counting   51

Cycle Counting Methodology: A Multifaceted Approach to Inventory Accuracy and Operational Efficiency   51

Inventory Discrepancy Resolution: An Indispensable Component of Strategic Inventory Management   52

Continuous Improvement in Inventory Accuracy: The Bedrock of Supply Chain Excellence   53

Importance of Inventory Accuracy   54

Chapter 7
Chapter 7: Supply Chain Collaboration and Vendor Managed Inventory (VMI)   55

Collaborative Relationships with Suppliers: A Bedrock for Optimising Inventory Management in a Volatile Market Environment   55

Vendor Managed Inventory: A Scholarly Exploration of its Benefits and Challenges   56

Implementing Vendor Managed Inventory Programs: A Comprehensive Guide   57

Continuous Improvement as a Cornerstone of Operational Excellence in Vendor Managed Inventory (VMI) Processes   58

Chapter 8
Chapter 8: Inventory Optimisation in E-commerce and Omni-channel Retailing   61

Unique Challenges in E-commerce Inventory Management   61

Multi-Channel Fulfillment Strategies: An Analytical Framework for the Integration and Optimisation of Diverse Sales Platforms   62

Inventory Allocation and Network Optimisation: A Synthesis of Best Practices for Supply Chain Efficiency   63

Inventory Management in the Age of Digital Marketplaces: A Multifaceted Exploration   64

Chapter 9
Chapter 9: Performance Metrics and KPIs for Inventory Management   67

Performance Metrics and Key Performance Indicators (KPIs) in Inventory Management   67

A Deeper Dive into Measuring Inventory Turnover   68

Fill Rate and Perfect Order Performance: Integral Components for Supply Chain Efficacy   69

Continuous Improvement through Performance Metrics: A Methodological Approach   70

Chapter 10
Chapter 10: Implementing Supply Chain Optimisation Strategies   71

Assessing Current Inventory Management Practices   71

Developing an Inventory Optimisation Strategy   72

Change Management and Implementation Challenges within Inventory Management   73

Monitoring and Continuous Improvement: The Bedrock of Optimisation   *74*

Chapter 11
Chapter 11: Empirical Analyses of Supply Chain Optimisation Strategies   *75*

Case Study 1: Augmenting Operational Efficiency through Sophisticated Demand Forecasting Mechanisms   *75*

Case Study 2: Implementing Just-In-Time (JIT) Inventory Management: A Critical Analysis of Operational Efficiency and Strategic Approaches   *76*

Case Study 3: Achieving Inventory Accuracy through Cycle Counting   *77*

Case Study 4: An Empirical Examination of a Collaborative Vendor Managed Inventory Success Story   *78*

Chapter 12
Chapter 12: Future Trends and Innovations in Inventory Management   *81*

The Incorporation of Automation and Robotics in Warehousing: A Multidisciplinary Approach to Optimising Inventory Management Systems   *81*

The Pervasiveness and Transformative Impact of the Internet of Things (IoT) on Inventory Optimisation in Contemporary Business Environments   *82*

Artificial Intelligence and Machine Learning Applications in Inventory Management: A Paradigmatic Shift in Analytical Capability and Operational Efficiency   *83*

Predictive Analytics for Inventory Management: A Paradigm Shift Towards Operational Excellence and Competitive Edge   *83*

Blockchain Technology as a Catalyst for Enhancing Supply Chain Transparency and Integrity   *85*

Augmented Reality and its Multifaceted Contributions to Order Picking Operations in Contemporary Inventory Management Systems   *85*

The Pioneering Role of Drone Technology in Reimagining Inventory Auditing Protocols   *86*

The Pervasiveness and Operational Imperatives of Mobile Technology in Real-Time Inventory Management   *86*

Sustainability in Inventory Management: From Trendy Nomenclature to Organisational Imperatives   *87*

Omni-Channel Inventory Management: A Comprehensive, Data-Driven Strategy for Operational Excellence and Consumer Engagement in a Multi-Channel Retail Ecosystem   *88*

Voice-Directed Warehousing: Reconceptualising Inventory Management Through Advanced Speech Recognition Systems   *88*

Additive Manufacturing in the Inventory Domain: A Comprehensive Examination of the Multifaceted Impacts of 3D Printing Technologies on Contemporary Production and Inventory Management Dynamic   *89*

Gamification in Inventory Management: An Innovative Pedagogical Approach to Augmenting Employee Productivity and Organisational Efficacy   *90*

Machine-to-Machine Communication in Inventory Management: A Comprehensive Examination of the Automation of Stock Control and Decision-making Processes through an Interdisciplinary Academic Le   *90*

Radio Frequency Identification (RFID) and Smart Shelves: Towards a Comprehensive Ontological Framework for Real-time Inventory Management in Complex Operational Environments   *91*

Data Analytics and Predictive Modeling: Customizing Inventory Metrics in Synchronization with Anticipated Consumer Behavioural Patterns: An Interdisciplinary Examination   *91*

Global and Distributed Inventory Systems: Challenges and Strategic Opportunities in a Globalised Economy   *92*

Cybersecurity in Inventory Management: Implications, Technologies, and Emerging Research Directions   *93*

Evolution of Self-Learning Capabilities in Modern Supply Chain Systems: A Computational Approach Leveraging Advanced Artificial Intelligence Algorithms in Predictive Analytics and Operational   *93*

The Emergence of Natural Language Processing in Supply Chain Data Analysis: A Comprehensive Examination of Linguistic Computational Models in Facilitating Intuitive Human-Machine Interfaces   94

The Integration of Collaborative Robots (Cobots) in Contemporary Inventory Management: A Comprehensive Multidisciplinary Study on Efficiency and Workplace Safety Paradigms   95

Quantum Computing for the Computational Advancement of Optimisation Problems in Inventory Management Systems   96

Chapter 13
Conclusion: Unlocking Efficiency through Inventory Management   97

Synthesis of Salient Concepts and Strategic Frameworks   97

The Imperative of Sustained Enhancement in Inventory Management: A Scholarly Perspective   98

A Scholarly Call to Action: Strategic Imperatives for Warehouse Managers and Inventory Practitioners in Modern Supply Chain Management   99

Appendix A: Glossary of Terms   101

Appendix B: Regulatory Landscape   105

Appendix C: Inventory Management Checklist   108

Appendix F: Typologies of Inventory: A Comprehensive Categorization   111

Appendix G: Styles of Inventory Management: A Scholarly Exploration   114

Appendix H: Comprehensive Analysis of Inventory Management Approaches, Evaluative Checklists, and Auditory Techniques in the Realm of E-Commerce   116

1. CHAPTER 1: INTRODUCTION TO SUPPLY CHAIN OPTIMISATION

Understanding the Fundamental Imperatives of Supply Chain Optimisation

In the intricate tapestry of today's globalised and fiercely competitive business environment, the optimisation of supply chains stands out as an indispensable component for the success matrix of warehouse overseers, inventory strategists, and practitioners within the domain of supply chain management. Ensuring adept management of inventory is paramount for enterprises not only to fulfil evolving customer expectations but also to achieve fiscal prudence and augmented operational proficiency. Within this subchapter, we embark on an analytical exploration of the salient significance of supply chain optimisation, with a concentrated lens on the intricate world of inventory management.

To begin our exploration, one must recognise the profound influence of supply chain optimisation on the very bedrock of business operations: customer contentment. In this contemporary era, characterised by ever-escalating consumer expectations, it is incumbent upon businesses to guarantee product availability with utmost precision in terms of timing and location. By meticulously optimising the supply chain, warehouse supervisors can ascertain judicious inventory equilibrium, thereby mitigating the dual challenges of stock-outs and superfluous inventory. Such strategic inventory control not only elevates service quality but also fosters enduring customer allegiance.

From a fiscal perspective, the optimisation of the supply chain is a pivotal instrument in curtailing operational costs. The economic implications of inventory holding, often under-appreciated, can weigh heavily on an organisation's financial health. By adopting and institutionalising astute inventory management methodologies—such as the Just-In-Time (JIT) inventory paradigms or intricate demand forecasting mechanisms—inventory stewards can judiciously curtail holding expenditures without endangering service benchmarks. Concurrently, a meticulously orchestrated supply chain presents myriad opportunities to refine processes, curtail procurement-to-delivery durations, and optimize logistics expenditures—cumulatively translating to substantial cost-efficiency.

Delving deeper into operational dynamics, it becomes evident that supply chain optimisation serves as a linchpin for bolstering operational prowess. An adeptly streamlined supply chain facilitates harmonious orchestration across its myriad phases, encompassing procurement, manufacturing, and the eventual distribution. Empowered by technological advancements and sophisticated data analytics, warehouse strategists can harness real-time insights into inventory nuances, consumer demand trajectories, and supplier efficacy. This facilitates informed, proactive strategising, optimising resource deployment, and ensuring agile adaptability. By assiduously addressing operational impediments and refining procedural flow, organisations can amplify productivity metrics, curtail procedural discrepancies, and elevate the holistic operational benchmark.

In the context of the modern business zeitgeist, marked by the proliferation of e-commerce and intricate globalisation patterns, supply chain intricacies have multiplied manifold. However, by assimilating and institutionalising optimisation protocols, inventory stewards can adeptly navigate these intricacies, preempt demand variances, and manage inventory across a diversified array of channels. This operational nimbleness and strategic foresight become the bulwarks ensuring an organisation's competitiveness, enabling it to maintain its vanguard position and capitalize on emergent market opportunities.

To encapsulate, the realm of supply chain optimisation emerges as a non-negotiable cornerstone for inventory strategists, warehouse overseers, and all affiliated with supply chain management. By internalising its pivotal significance, enterprises can not only delight their customer base but also achieve operational and fiscal excellence, fortifying their stature in a volatile and competitive business landscape.

Key Concepts and Definitions: A Deep Dive

In the intricate mosaic of supply chain optimisation and inventory management, possessing a robust grasp of the foundational lexicon is not just beneficial but paramount. This subchapter endeavours to furnish Warehouse Managers, Inventory Strategists, and professionals navigating the vast arena of Supply Chain Management with a nuanced, comprehensive exposition of these pivotal terminologies.

- **Inventory Management:** At its core, inventory management encapsulates the methodologies employed to supervise and regulate the ingress, egress, and stowage of merchandise within a warehouse or a distribution node. This complex choreography requires astute synchronisation of supply vis-a-vis demand, meticulous stock level calibration, and prudent fiscal oversight. The overarching objective remains unwavering: ensuring product accessibility aligns seamlessly with consumer requisitions.
- **Stock Keeping Unit (SKU):** An SKU, often envisioned as the DNA fingerprint of inventory items, is a distinctive alphanumeric code ascribed to a singular item or product iteration within an inventory spectrum. This microscopic granularity permits warehouse curators and inventory custodians to pinpoint, surveil, and orchestrate individual items' movement, thereby enhancing precision across the supply chain continuum.
- **Lead Time:** Lead time, in essence, is the temporal span stretching from the genesis of an order to its culminating fulfilment or delivery. This duration assimilates diverse phases such as order assimilation, manufacturing cadence, transit timeframes, and other contributory elements that shape the aggregate product delivery trajectory. A profound appreciation of lead time is instrumental for calibrated inventory prognostication and astute demand anticipation.
- **Safety Stock:** Envisioned as the buffer or cushion layer in inventory paradigms, safety stock is deliberately curated inventory that transcends conventional stock thresholds. This reservoir exists to insulate operations against unpredictable demand surges or potential disruptions permeating the supply chain. It's the armor shielding businesses from the precariousness of stockouts, ensuring consistent product availability amidst volatile scenarios.
- **Economic Order Quantity (EOQ):** EOQ stands as a mathematical beacon, guiding businesses to discern the quintessential order volume that concurrently minimizes holistic inventory-associated expenditures. These include

the financial implications of inventory sustenance (holding costs) and the economic footprint of order placements (ordering costs). Through the EOQ prism, businesses can tread the fine line between excess inventory burdens and recurrent order overheads, thus achieving optimal inventory equipoise.

- **Just-in-Time (JIT):** An embodiment of lean inventory orchestration, the Just-in-Time philosophy champions the minimalist approach. It underscores the principle of introducing and processing goods strictly aligned with their immediate requisition either in the production arena or responding to customer solicitations. JIT, as a strategy, attenuates inventory maintenance expenditures, simultaneously augmenting supply chain agility and operational nimbleness.

- **Demand Forecasting:** This is the prescient art and science of calibrating prospective consumer appetite for distinct products or services. By sculpting accurate demand prognostications, inventory stewards can finetune stock thresholds, curtail inventory redundancies, and cater to consumer exigencies with heightened efficiency.

By immersing themselves in this enriched lexicon, Warehouse Managers, Inventory Strategists, and connoisseurs of Supply Chain Management are better poised to fathom the depth of inventory management's intricacies. Armed with this knowledge, they can architect and execute strategies that elevate supply chain potency to its zenith.

Benefits of Efficient Inventory Management within the Supply Chain Framework

In the intricate web of supply chain management, efficient inventory management emerges as a linchpin in ensuring optimal operations and strategic positioning. Within the tapestry of the '**Mastering the Chain: A Comprehensive Guide to Elevating Efficiency through Strategic Inventory Management**,' this subchapter delves deep into the multifaceted advantages accrued from instituting proficient inventory management protocols across diverse industrial domains.

- **Mitigation of Holding Costs:** At the forefront of the benefits is the pronounced reduction in holding costs. Efficient inventory management is a strategic approach wherein optimal inventory levels are maintained to forestall excessive accumulation of stock. Such excessive stockpiling inadvertently triggers spiralling costs related to storage, insurance, and handling. The nuanced approach of efficient inventory management aids businesses in striking a harmonious equilibrium between satiating customer demand and precluding stock overflow, paving the way for noteworthy fiscal prudence.

- **Augmentation of Customer Satisfaction:** In the dynamic business landscape, customer-centricity is paramount. Efficient inventory management serves as a conduit to bolster customer satisfaction levels. By assuring the perennial availability of products congruent with customer timelines, businesses can adeptly cater to customer exigencies. This not only truncates lead times but also amplifies customer satisfaction quotients, fostering enhanced customer allegiance and catalysing recurrent patronage. An additional advantage materializes in the aversion of stock-outs, thereby safeguarding against missed revenue streams and potential reputational hazards.

- **Enhancement in Forecasting Precision:** Drawing insights from historical datasets and discernible demand trajectories, efficient inventory management capacitates businesses with heightened forecasting precision. Such meticulous forecasting engenders superior inventory planning and harmonisation, facilitating inventory custodians to synchronise their logistical undertakings with projected demand, thereby mitigating the dual perils of excessive stock and stock paucity.

- **Refinement in Order Fulfilment Metrics:** Rooted in the paradigm of data-driven decision-making, efficient inventory management empowers businesses with granular inventory data, culminating in expedited order diagnosis and subsequent fulfilment. This dual advantage not only accentuates customer gratification levels but also engenders operational streamlining, concurrently paring down the fiscal implications linked to protracted order processing intervals.

- **Strategic Supply Chain Network Optimisation:** Venturing beyond the confines of mere inventory, efficient inventory management furnishes businesses with the analytical tools to recalibrate their supply chain frameworks. By deciphering inventory metrics juxtaposed with demand oscillations, potential avenues emerge for inventory consolidation, streamlining, or strategic realignment across a multitude of locales. This orchestration engenders elevated transport and warehousing efficacy, truncated lead times, and a holistic uplift in supply chain vitality.

- **Fostering Informed Decision-making Matrix:** The contemporary business environment mandates real-time decision-making prowess. Endowed with instantaneous access to inventory matrices, stakeholders spanning from warehouse supervisors to supply chain maestros can instantiate judicious choices encompassing procurement paradigms, production stratagems, and inventory rejuvenation protocols. This alacrity not only bolsters operational fluency but also positions businesses to seamlessly navigate the ever-fluctuating market topographies.

In encapsulation, the multifarious advantages accruing from efficient inventory management stand as a testament to its cardinal role within the supply chain construct. From fiscal savings and customer centricity to strategic alignment and real-time decision-making agility, proficient inventory management emerges as an indispensable catalyst in engendering supply chain excellence.

2. CHAPTER 2: FUNDAMENTALS OF INVENTORY MANAGEMENT

The Pivotal Role of Inventory in Supply Chain Dynamics

The multifaceted role of inventory within the expansive realm of supply chain management cannot be underscored enough. Its meticulous and strategic management serves as the linchpin for the seamless operation of warehouse functions and processes. This subchapter delves into the profound implications of inventory within the supply chain framework, elucidating ways to hone it for optimum efficiency.

Inventory, in its essence, serves as a stabilising buffer, deftly mediating between the oscillating forces of demand and supply. This intermediary role guarantees an ample supply to satiate customer needs, mitigating the risks associated with stock-outs and the consequential erosion of sales. By astutely positioning inventory across the continuum of the supply chain, warehouse professionals can precipitate shorter lead times and foster heightened levels of customer satisfaction. Beyond its primary role, inventory is instrumental in counterbalancing the vagaries and unpredictabilities inherent in both demand and supply. This flexibility empowers organisations to nimbly adapt to capricious market trends and evolving consumer inclinations.

A salient advantage embedded within proficient inventory management is the potential for fiscal optimisation. A surfeit of inventory inadvertently immobilises precious capital resources and induces ancillary storage expenditures. Conversely, a scant inventory regime can be the harbinger of missed sales opportunities and disgruntled customers. The challenge for warehouse overseers is to calibrate the optimal equilibrium, and this is achievable through the deployment of nuanced inventory control stratagems such as predictive demand forecasting, prudent safety stock governance, and judicious order quantity calibration. Through assiduously gauging demand trajectories, warehouse strategists can pare down holding expenses whilst ensuring punctual stock revitalisation.

The intricacies of inventory management are inextricably interlaced with other supply chain segments, including but not limited to procurement, manufacturing, and logistical transportation. Synchronised orchestration amongst these facets is imperative to circumvent operational impediments and to elevate the overarching supply chain efficacy. As an exemplar, precise demand prognostication can synchronise production cadences, thereby truncating production gestation periods and curtailing the incidence of stock-outs. In a parallel vein, streamlined transportation and expedited delivery modalities are quintessential to ascertain that inventory is dispatched to its intended destination in a punctual manner.

The contemporary era has witnessed a technological renaissance that has imparted transformative innovations to inventory management protocols. Warehouse stewards can harness sophisticated inventory management digital suites and analytical tools to introduce automation into realms like demand anticipation, order trajectory monitoring, and periodic inventory rejuvenation. These avant-garde solutions proffer real-time transparency into inventory matrices, facilitating prescient decision-making and diminishing the peril associated with inventory scarcities or surpluses.

To encapsulate, the art and science of inventory management are central to the fine-tuning of supply chain mechanisms. Custodians of warehouses and inventory connoisseurs are tasked with the monumental responsibility of harmonising the dual forces of supply and demand, exploiting technological advancements, and forging synergies with allied supply chain sectors. By embracing and refining these inventory management tenets, enterprises can amplify customer delight, curtail superfluous expenses, and usher in unprecedented efficiency into their supply chain orchestration.

Types of Inventories in Strategic Supply Chain Management

Within the purview of supply chain management, inventory serves as the reservoir of goods and materials that an enterprise retains, fulfilling various operational and strategic purposes. The meticulous management of this inventory stands as a pivotal element, not only to bolster efficiency but also to curtail ancillary costs that burgeon within a warehouse or a broader supply chain framework. Grasping the nuances and complexities of the different categories of inventory becomes imperative for warehouse managers, inventory specialists, and supply chain management professionals, enabling them to render data-driven decisions and instate robust inventory management paradigms.

- **Raw Materials:** At the foundational level of any production continuum lie the raw materials. These are unprocessed, basic elements that are poised for transformation into finished goods. Examples span from metals to chemicals, fabrics, and an array of other rudimentary constituents. The onus rests on warehouse managers to perpetually ascertain a consistent influx of these raw materials, thus ensuring that the production pipelines remain devoid of any unforeseen disruptions or lags.

- **Work-in-Progress (WIP):** Representing an intermediary phase within the production trajectory, the work-in-progress inventory is emblematic of goods that are yet to reach their culmination. Quantitatively, WIP inventory encapsulates the fiscal value tethered to the raw materials, labor exertions, and overhead expenditures embroiled in the manufacturing conduit. The astute management of WIP is pivotal to preempt potential bottlenecks and to underpin an uninterrupted production cadence.

- **Finished Goods:** Serving as the epitome of the production sequence, finished goods are the consummate products primed for sale or subsequent distribution. The challenge for warehouse managers is to adeptly anticipate market demands, thereby calibrating the quantum of finished goods inventory. An over-accumulation might escalate carrying costs, whereas a deficit could compromise sales and tarnish customer relations.

- **Maintenance, Repair, and Operations (MRO):** The MRO inventory encompasses a spectrum of items pivotal for the sustenance of operational continuity. This includes, but is not limited to, tools, ancillary parts, and assorted supplies. The strategic calibration of MRO inventory is essential, ensuring operational fluidity without inadvertently immobilising valuable working capital.

- **Safety Stock:** As a safeguard against the unpredictable undulations of market demand or potential disruptions in the supply chain, safety stock serves as a provisional buffer. In determining the requisite volume of safety stock, warehouse managers must judiciously weigh parameters such as procurement lead time, the oscillations in demand, and incumbent service level commitments.

- **Consignment Inventory:** This unique inventory classification is delineated by an arrangement where the stock, though belonging to a supplier, is ensconced at the customer's facility. It remains there until requisitioned for consumption or sale. This logistical maneuver can be economically advantageous for the customer by truncating carrying costs, while concurrently ensuring that suppliers maintain a consistent supply conduit. However, the success of this model is contingent upon rigorous inventory oversight and synergised coordination to obviate potential discrepancies or stock depletions.

In summation, a profound understanding and strategic categorisation of inventory types empower warehouse and inventory management professionals. This foundational knowledge facilitates the formulation of judicious inventory strategies, optimising fiscal outlays, safeguarding against stock voids, and augmenting the holistic efficiency of operational workflows.

Inventory Costs and Trade-offs: Navigating the Economic Landscape of Supply Chain Management

Inventory management, a cornerstone of supply chain optimisation, holds paramount importance in the overarching success trajectory of any commercial enterprise. For professionals helming warehouse management, inventory oversight, and broader supply chain strategies, it is indispensable to delve deep into the multifaceted realm of inventory costs and the inherent trade-offs. This subchapter endeavors to illuminate the intricate tapestry of costs bound to inventory and the judicious trade-offs warranting contemplation to achieve equilibrium.

Inventory Costs

- **Holding (Carrying) Costs:** At the core of inventory expenses lies the holding or carrying costs, which encapsulate the financial outlays tied to the storage of inventory items. This includes, but is not limited to, warehousing rent, utility charges, insurance premiums, and labor compensation. With the prolongation of inventory stasis within the warehouse, these holding costs witness a surge. Thus, it becomes imperative for warehouse managers to meticulously calibrate inventory volumes, mitigating these expenses while preserving stellar customer service standards.

- **Ordering Costs:** Ordering costs signify the financial implications of the act of procurement. These manifest in the form of administrative expenditures, transportation-related costs, and charges levied by suppliers. Through the strategic modulation of order magnitudes and cadences, inventory professionals can curtail ordering costs, concurrently ensuring a consistent reservoir of requisite goods.

- **Stockout Costs:** The financial repercussions of inventory depletion, termed as stockout costs, are multifarious. They span lost sales opportunities, potential customer attrition, and dents to the brand's reputation. The task for inventory managers is to weave a delicate balance, navigating the treacherous waters between escalating holding costs and the perils of stockout.

- **Obsolescence Costs:** The spectre of obsolescence looms large, with dormant inventory items running the risk of becoming technologically redundant, surpassing their shelf life, or witnessing evaporating market demand. Such obsolescence can be a drain on financial resources. It is, thus, incumbent upon inventory stewards to perpetually refresh and refine their inventory repositories, excising items teetering on obsolescence.

Trade-offs in Inventory Management

- **Service Level vs. Holding Costs:** Elevating the service level pinnacle, through the bolstering of inventory caches, indeed truncates stockout risks. However, this amplification simultaneously swells holding costs. The conundrum for warehouse maestros lies in orchestrating a symphony between customer gratification and the financial burdens of inventory.

- **Lead Time vs. Holding Costs:** A diminution in lead time can indeed shave off holding expenses. However, this contraction might necessitate augmented inventory stocks, counterbalancing truncated replenishment intervals. The crucible for supply chain experts is in discerning the equilibrium between the virtues of lead time compression and the fiscal ramifications of inventory.

- **Economies of Scale vs. Ordering Costs:** Procurement in voluminous quantities can unlock economies of scale, ushering in diminished per-unit expenses. Paradoxically, this amplification can spike ordering costs. The onus is on inventory strategists to dissect the dichotomy between ordering expenditures and the allure of scale-driven economic advantages.

The mastery over the myriad inventory costs and their concomitant trade-offs empowers warehouse custodians, inventory architects, and supply chain aficionados to sculpt optimised, efficiency-driven inventory paradigms. To foster both operational efficiency and profitability, it becomes quintessential to strike a harmonious balance amidst holding, ordering, stockout, and obsolescence costs. By assiduously evaluating these interplays, commercial entities can unfurl the latent prowess of their supply chain matrix, fortifying their competitive stature in the ever-evolving marketplace.

Inventory Control Techniques: A Scholarly Dive into Operational Efficacy

In the intricate web of organisational operations, inventory control emerges as a linchpin, tethering an organisation's supply chain prowess to its commercial success. At its core, inventory control masterfully choreographs the ballet of commodities, transitioning seamlessly from suppliers to end consumers, all while orchestrating an equilibrium between cost-effectiveness, client gratification, and optimal stock levels. This subchapter endeavours to shed light on a compendium of inventory control methodologies, offering invaluable insights for warehouse chieftains, inventory strategists, and supply chain maestros, to bolster their operational acumen.

- **ABC Analysis:** Embarking on the realm of ABC Analysis, one dives deep into the stratification of inventory items, segmented into triadic categories, hinged on both monetary worth and utility frequency. The 'Class A' echelon represents the crème de la crème of inventory, distinguished by their elevated value and recurrent utilisation, necessitating rigorous oversight and perpetual audits. 'Class B' straddles the middle ground, encapsulating items of moderate value and usage, meriting commensurate vigilance. The 'Class C' compartment, conversely, houses low-value, sporadically-used items, amenable to lenient supervision. This hierarchical delineation empowers managers to judiciously allocate organisational resources, tailoring their oversight intensity to the pertinence of the inventory items.

- **Just-in-Time (JIT):** Embracing the JIT paradigm, organisations commit to a Spartan inventory ethos, orchestrating the timely influx of commodities in congruence with production exigencies or consumer requisitions. This minimisation of stock reservoirs translates into diminished holding expenditures and invigorated fiscal liquidity. Nevertheless, JIT's efficacy is contingent on an immaculately synchronised supply chain and profound supplier symbiosis, ensuring punctual consignments.

- **Economic Order Quantity (EOQ):** The EOQ model is a consummate marriage of mathematical precision and inventory strategy. It prescribes the quintessential procurement volume, harmonising the duality of holding and ordering financial implications. By leveraging EOQ, custodians of inventory can pinpoint the procurement sweet spot, sidestepping the pitfalls of stock inadequacy and superfluity, consequently elevating operational thriftiness, and proficiency.

- **Vendor-Managed Inventory (VMI):** VMI is a testament to the power of collaborative synergy. Here, the baton of inventory management at the client's precincts is passed to the supplier. Fortified by real-time data accessibility and entrusted with replenishment obligations, suppliers metamorphose into proactive partners, ensuring the ubiquity of pertinent products. VMI's embrace can catalyse the diminution of stock deficiencies, optimize order logistics, and enhance the holistic vitality of the supply chain.

- **Safety Stock:** In an unpredictable commercial landscape, safety stock emerges as a protective bulwark, cushioning organisations against the volatility of demand oscillations or unforeseen supply chain hiccups. By astutely calibrating safety stock thresholds, grounded in historical analytics and procurement timelines, strategists can guarantee a steadfast commodity supply, satiating clientele requisitions.

In summation, the adroit adoption and adaptation of these inventory control archetypes can transmute organisational inventory stewardship from a mundane chore into a strategic tour de force. However, it is of quintessential importance that decision-makers judiciously evaluate their unique organizational contours and the market's capricious temperament, ensuring their inventory strategies remain both resilient and responsive.

3. CHAPTER 3: FORECASTING AND DEMAND PLANNING

The Imperative of Precise Demand Forecasting in Modern Inventory Management

In the intricate tapestry of inventory management, the precision of demand forecasting emerges as an indispensable cornerstone for streamlining supply chain operations. It's no hyperbole to state that the cogs of this vast machinery — from warehouse overseers to inventory strategists, and the legion of supply chain management professionals — revolve around the pivotal axis of demand prediction. The repercussions of this function echo across the spectrum, influencing inventory thresholds, dictating customer contentment metrics, and shaping the financial outcomes of the enterprise.

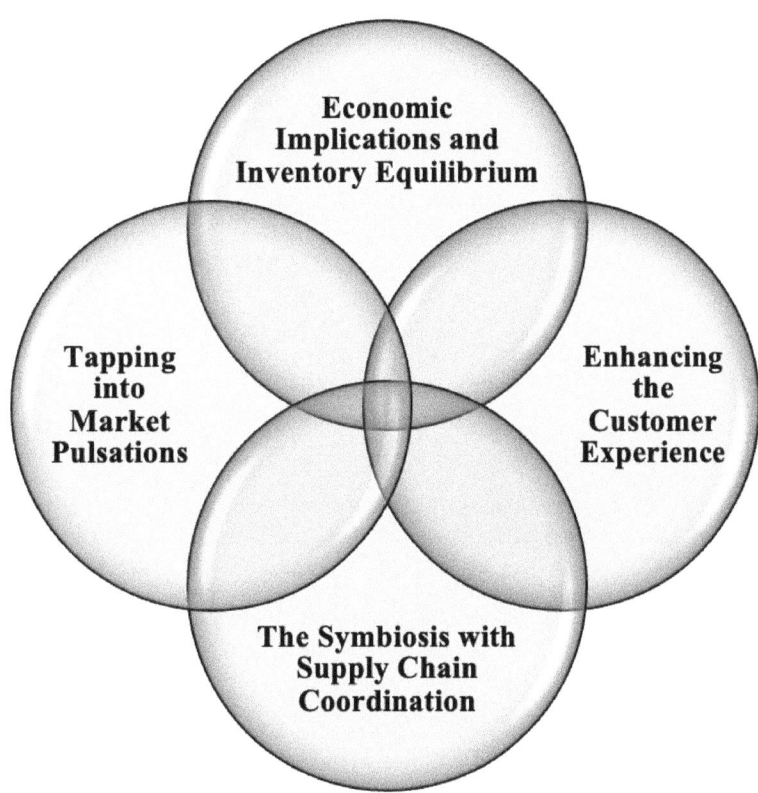

Figure 1 : The Imperative of Precise Demand Forecasting in Modern Inventory Management

- **Economic Implications and Inventory Equilibrium:** Precise demand forecasting is a beacon that illuminates the pathway to inventory equilibrium. Businesses, by tapping into the power of accurate demand predictions, can ascertain the ideal volume of commodities to procure. This judicious approach aids in curtailing the twin pitfalls of overstocking and stock-outs, thereby sidestepping the fiscal ramifications of inflated inventory holdings and the ancillary costs. The resultant effects are manifold: an augmentation of cash liquidity, a downturn in the perils of inventory becoming passé, and a streamlined warehousing strategy wherein storage space is judiciously allocated to mirror product demand, obviating the clamor for superfluous warehousing expanses.

- **Enhancing the Customer Experience:** The nexus between meticulous demand forecasting and customer contentment is unequivocal. By deciphering the often-elusive patterns of consumer demand, businesses can perpetuate a state of inventory harmony, thereby minimising the specters of stock depletions and lagging backorders. This not only bolsters customer allegiance but also galvanizes the brand's stature in the market. The cascade effect is an uptick in sales trajectories.

- **The Symbiosis with Supply Chain Coordination:** For supply chain management aficionados, accurate demand intel is the linchpin that fosters a seamless synergy with suppliers. Armed with incisive demand insights, these professionals can fine tune collaborations, ensuring that deliveries adhere to a clockwork precision, thus curtailing protracted lead times. The ramifications are profound, catalysing efficient production schema, judicious resource delegation, and the obviation of production snags, all converging to heighten operational veracity.

- **Tapping into Market Pulsations:** One of the unsung merits of astute demand forecasting is its potential as a barometer to gauge market oscillations and evolving consumer proclivities. With a judicious amalgamation of retrospective sales analysis, market milieu assessment, and an understanding of external catalysts, businesses are equipped to preempt future demand vacillations. This vantage point facilitates a nimbleness in strategy recalibration, ensuring businesses are not just reactive but proactive, granting them a competitive edge and a keenness to capitalize on emergent market avenues.

To transmute the theoretical potential of demand forecasting into tangible outcomes, it's imperative for businesses to harness the prowess of cutting-edge technological modalities. The troika of machine learning paradigms, artificial intelligence frameworks, and prescient analytics emerge as invaluable assets. By embedding these technological marvels into inventory management ecosystems, the triad of warehouse directors, inventory tacticians, and supply chain maestros can elevate decision-making acumen, refine forecasting fidelity, and calibrate inventory matrices to perfection.

In the final reckoning, the message is unambiguous. The gravitas of immaculate demand forecasting in inventory management cannot be overstated. For those at the helm — warehouse chieftains, inventory architects, and supply chain connoisseurs — a recognition of this doctrine is non-negotiable. It's the bedrock of operational finesse, fiscal prudence, customer elation, and market competitiveness. With the judicious infusion of avant-garde technologies and analytical acumen, businesses stand poised to actualize the zenith of demand forecasting precision, and by extension, supply chain mastery.

Techniques for Demand Forecasting

Within the intricate matrix of inventory management, demand forecasting emerges as the linchpin that propels supply chain efficiency to its zenith. By assiduously prognosticating customer requisites, a cohort comprising warehouse stewards, inventory strategists, and supply chain mavens can meticulously calibrate their decisions, spanning inventory thresholds, production timetables, and distribution blueprints. The ensuing discourse delves deep into a pantheon of demand forecasting methodologies, each promising to augment inventory management paradigms and, in turn, elevate the overarching supply chain orchestration.

- **Time Series Analysis:** Heralded as a venerable forecasting paradigm, Time Series Analysis harnesses the potency of historical data, employing it as the crucible to distill patterns and evolutionary trajectories in demand. Within the arsenal of warehouse overseers, statistical constructs like moving averages and exponential smoothing emerge as invaluable tools, facilitating the extrapolation of future demand nuances predicated on retrospective sales intel. Time series dissection bequeaths inventory tacticians with a foundational forecasting template, one that is malleable enough to accommodate seasonal oscillations, evolutionary trends, and a mosaic of pertinent determinants.

- **Market Research and Surveys:** An expedition into the domain of market research and solicitation of surveys unveils a treasure trove of insights – discerning consumer predilections, purchasing comportments, and prospective demand oscillations. Warehouse directors can amalgamate their efforts with marketing cognoscenti to mine data, shedding light on consumer currents, competitive landscape analyses, and market kinetics. This qualitative reconnaissance dovetails seamlessly with its quantitative counterparts, elucidating external catalysts poised to shape demand contours.

- **Collaborative Planning, Forecasting, and Replenishment (CPFR):** The CPFR paradigm champions the doctrine of data symbiosis, wherein intel germane to demand is seamlessly shared across the supply chain continuum - encompassing suppliers, distributors, and the end consumer. Such an integrated approach bequeaths warehouse strategists with a panoramic view of the supply chain tableau, culminating in demand forecasts of unparalleled precision. The real genius of CPFR lies in its mitigation of the notorious bullwhip oscillations, heralding a new era of anticipatory inventory management that staunchly curtails both stock redundancies and deficiencies.

- **Machine Learning and Artificial Intelligence (AI):** The digital renaissance, characterized by exponential strides in technology, has ushered in an era where machine learning matrices and AI algorithms dissect voluminous datasets, unearthing intricate patterns and pre-empting demand with uncanny precision. Warehouse custodians, armed with these avant-garde methodologies, can embark on a deep dive into historical sales archives, consumer behavior patterns, market fluctuations, and even exogenous stimuli like meteorological shifts or the zeitgeist captured on social media platforms. The dynamism inherent in machine learning algorithms ensures a continuous evolutionary trajectory, refining forecasting fidelity with each iteration.

- **Demand Sensing:** Operating at the confluence of immediacy and precision, Demand Sensing harnesses real-time data streams emanating from diverse conduits, be it point-of-sale ecosystems, the digital hum of social media, or online commerce platforms. By maintaining a vigilant watch over these pulsating demand conduits, warehouse maestros can rapidly recalibrate their strategies in the face of shifting consumer appetites or market metamorphoses. This technique promises a fluidic approach to inventory stewardship, ensuring alignment with the mercurial whims of real-time demand.

The judicious application of the demand forecasting alchemies has the potential to transmute the very fabric of inventory management. For warehouse chieftains, inventory orchestrators, and supply chain aficionados, these methodologies beckon a future where inventory equilibria are achieved, stock voids become a rarity, and the economic implications of inventory holding are minimised. By harnessing the transformative power of demand forecasting, the horizon promises a supply chain operating at peak efficiency, delighting customers, and engendering fiscal prosperity.

Collaborative Demand Planning

In the intricate tapestry of supply chain management, inventory management emerges as a pivotal cog, orchestrating the uninterrupted transference of goods and fulfilling the intricate lattice of customer exigencies. Amidst the myriad strategies that have punctuated the landscape of supply chain logistics, collaborative demand planning has burgeoned, carving a niche for itself as an indispensable paradigm. This discourse seeks to elucidate the nuanced architecture of collaborative demand planning, spotlighting its indispensability for the triumvirate of warehouse curators, inventory strategists, and supply chain luminaries in the inventory management arena.

Collaborative demand planning can be distilled into a symphonic process that choreographs the concerted efforts of diverse stakeholders embedded in the supply chain continuum. The annals of traditional demand planning were often marred by insular operations, with the forecasting echelon shouldering the onus of prediction. This modus operandi occasionally birthed chasms between anticipated demand and the tangible requisites of customers. Contrarily, collaborative demand planning champions the dissolution of these operational bastions, kindling a cross-functional camaraderie wherein stakeholders synchronise their endeavours towards a unified vision.

Mobilising the acumen of warehouse overseers, inventory maestros, and supply chain virtuosos in the demand planning matrix can pave the way for demand forecasts of unparalleled precision. Warehouse custodians, wielding an intimate knowledge of inventory granularities, emerge as beacons, illuminating the landscape of stock purview. Concurrently, inventory tacticians, adept in dissecting historical data tapestries and distilling trends, bring their analytical prowess to the fore. Complementing this ensemble, supply chain aficionados, armed with a panoramic vantage of the entire supply chain tapestry, infuse the narrative with external determinants, ranging from the mercurial temperament of market dynamics to overarching economic pulses.

The dividends of collaborative demand planning are multifarious. Primarily, it heralds an era of augmented customer contentment, underpinned by the enhanced fidelity of demand forecasts that subsequently transmutes into optimal inventory readiness and diminished stock voids. Secondarily, this paradigm facilitates the meticulous calibration of inventory thresholds, ensuring their alignment with tangible demand, thereby curtailing inventory surpluses and the concomitant fiscal burdens of holding. Tertiarily, the spirit of collaboration ignites an ethos of transparency and mutual trust amongst the stakeholder fraternity, catalysing sagacious decision-making and attenuating discord.

To transmute the vision of collaborative demand planning into tangible reality, enterprises must channel investments into state-of-the-art technological infrastructures, platforms that champion real-time data symbiosis, interdisciplinary collaboration, and seamless integration across functional silos. Supplementing this digital foundation, the establishment of regular confluences and the institutionalisation of unfettered communication conduits is imperative, ensuring an incessant data interchange and feedback cadence.

In summation, the doctrine of collaborative demand planning emerges as a lighthouse for the vanguards of inventory management and the broader supply chain symphony. By orchestrating a harmonious ballet involving warehouse guardians, inventory strategists, and supply chain savants in the demand planning odyssey, enterprises can hone their forecasting precision, refine inventory equilibria, and subsequently amplify customer delight. The embrace of collaborative demand planning promises to be the panacea, rejuvenating inventory management protocols, amplifying fiscal returns, and ensuring an indomitable presence in the capricious theatre of modern commerce.

Demand Variability and Safety Stock

Within the intricate nexus of inventory management, the phenomenon of demand variability emerges as a cardinal determinant, profoundly influencing the trajectory of a supply chain's triumphs or tribulations. For the echelons of warehouse overseers, inventory tacticians, and supply chain connoisseurs, an intimate comprehension of demand variability is not merely advantageous but imperative, with its tendrils reaching deep into the very fabric of their operational modus operandi. This discourse endeavours to unravel the intricate dance between demand variability and safety stock, illuminating pathways to sculpt inventory management strategies that gracefully navigate the tempestuous seas of capricious demand matrices.

At its core, demand variability is the embodiment of oscillations in consumer requisition for a distinct product, spanning a delineated temporal arc. This flux is molded by a mélange of catalysts, from the rhythmic undulations of seasonality, the ebb and flow of market zeitgeists, the overarching tenor of economic landscapes, to even the abrupt and often cataclysmic upheavals instigated by phenomena such as natural cataclysms. Recognising the nuances of demand variability is not merely an academic exercise; it is a vital compass, with its readings echoing through inventory echelons and reverberating across the continuum of supply chain efficiency.

To buffer against the vicissitudes birthed by demand variability, the doctrine of safety stock emerges as a beacon. Conceived as supplementary inventory reserves, safety stock is that strategic bulwark against the surges of unanticipated demand or the turbidities of supply perturbations. Through judicious calibration of safety stock, the guardians of warehouses can weave a tapestry of assurance, ensuring that their inventory arsenals remain robust and poised to satiate customer solicitations, even when confronted with demand tempests or supply chain adversities.

The art and science of curating an optimal safety stock reservoir demand a meticulous exploration of demand architectures, necessitating reflections upon elements such as procurement lead times, order cadences, and the zeniths of service aspirations. Those at the helm of warehouses and inventory must choreograph a delicate ballet; on one end lies the need for a robust safety stock buffer to preclude inventory voids, while on the other end, the spectre of surplus inventory looms, with its talons threatening to ensnare capital and amplify overheads.

In the ensuing sections of this subchapter, we shall embark on an intellectual odyssey, navigating the myriad methodologies and paradigms instrumental in sculpting safety stock—ranging from foundational formulaic blueprints, the sagacity of statistical methodologies, to the avant-garde realms of probabilistic modeling. Each modality, with its unique strengths and constraints, will be juxtaposed against pragmatic exemplars, offering a tangible glimpse into their applicability within the crucible of real-world scenarios.

Moreover, our discourse will traverse the realms of demand forecasting precision and its intimate liaison with safety stock architectures. The alchemy of accurate demand foresight is pivotal, not merely as a tool but as a keystone, orchestrating inventory symphonies and attenuating the shadows of uncertainty. An exposition on diverse forecasting tapestries will ensue, underscoring the imperative of symbiotic dialogues and data confluences amongst the myriad stakeholders embroidering the supply chain.

As we culminate this subchapter, it is our aspiration that the trinity of warehouse custodians, inventory strategists, and supply chain luminaries emerge enlightened, with their intellectual reservoirs enriched. Armed with this refined understanding of demand variability and safety stock, they stand poised to sculpt strategies that meld both sagacity and pragmatism, ensuring that the supply chain machine operates with both precision and grace, invariably leading to an elevation in customer delight.

4. CHAPTER 4: INVENTORY OPTIMIZATION MODELS

Economic Order Quantity (EOQ) Model: A Critical Analysis

The Economic Order Quantity (EOQ) model stands as an indispensable pillar in the vast expanse of inventory management literature. Its foundational significance in streamlining supply chain operations cannot be overstated. As custodians of the supply chain—be they warehouse managers, inventory supervisors, or the larger contingent of supply chain management experts—it becomes imperative to have a nuanced understanding of the EOQ model. By leveraging its principles, these professionals can adeptly calibrate the delicate equilibrium between associated inventory expenditures and the requisite customer service benchmarks.

At its core, the EOQ model pivots on the assertion that an optimal ordering quantum exists—a quantity which, when ordered, diminishes the total expenses associated with inventory management to its nadir. Such expenditures bifurcate into two broad categories:

- **Carrying Costs:** These are inherent costs associated with retaining inventory over periods. They envelop expenses related to storage, ensuring the inventory against potential risks, managing obsolescence, and so on.

- **Ordering Costs:** These are the expenses incurred during the acquisition phase of inventory, encompassing administrative paperwork, logistical charges like transportation, and sundry processing overheads.

The discernment of the appropriate EOQ is pivotal in forestalling the dual pitfalls of overstocking and understocking—each presenting its own financial quandaries. Excess inventory commitment can immobilise vital capital, escalating the carrying costs, whereas inventory deficiencies can culminate in stock-outs—a scenario dreaded for its adverse customer implications and the consequential potential haemorrhage of revenue.

To decipher the EOQ, the model contemplates three cardinal parameters: the annual demand forecast, the per-order cost structure, and the annualised unit carrying cost. The quintessence of the EOQ formula emanates from harmonising the dichotomy between the aforementioned ordering and carrying costs.

By harnessing the insights proffered by the EOQ model, custodians of the warehouse can not only fine-tune inventory echelons but also exercise discernment in delineating reorder thresholds and batch quantities. This strategic implementation can engender an inventory landscape where the reservoirs are adequate to satiate customer exigencies yet remain cost-efficient.

However, a salient caveat accompanies the EOQ model—it operates within the constraints of specific presumptions, including but not limited to, invariable demand, predetermined and un-fluctuating cost regimes, and the non-applicability of volume discounts. Given these inherent assumptions, it becomes paramount for inventory stewards to perpetually reassess and recalibrate their EOQ extrapolations, factoring in the fluidity of market landscapes and evolving commercial matrices.

In an era where data is revered as the new oil, effectual deployment of the EOQ model mandates rigorous data acquisition and analytical rigor. It behooves warehouse supervisors to be armed with veracious, contemporaneous intel on demand trajectories, procurement lead times, and the nuanced cost anatomy. With the advent of avant-garde technologies and sophisticated analytical instruments, such data can be assimilated and the EOQ tenets applied with augmented precision.

To encapsulate, the EOQ model, in its intricate design, offers a panacea for inventory conundrums faced by warehouse overseers, inventory pundits, and the overarching domain of supply chain aficionados. A judicious appropriation of this model can catalyze unparalleled efficiencies in inventory oversight, elevate customer satisfaction matrices, and provide a fillip to the holistic performance of supply chains.

Reorder Point (ROP) Model: A Quantitative Framework for Strategic Inventory Optimisation

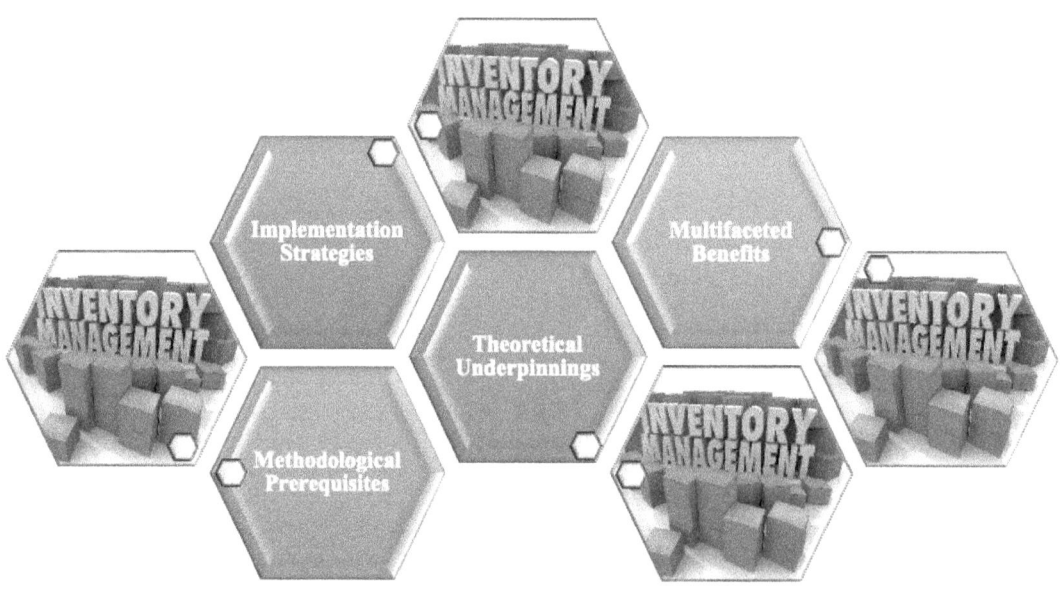

Figure 2 : Reorder Point (ROP) model

In the intricate landscape of inventory management, a perpetual dilemma that plagues warehouse managers, inventory coordinators, and supply chain strategists is the precarious balancing act of optimising inventory levels. Overstocking, while offering the reassurance of meeting unexpected demand spikes, imposes tangible economic burdens—constraining liquidity, escalating holding costs, and amplifying the risk of inventory obsolescence. Conversely, under-stocking is fraught with its own litany of perils—missed revenue opportunities, deteriorating customer satisfaction, and tarnished brand equity. This quandary positions the Reorder Point (ROP) model as an indispensable analytical tool that systematically guides businesses in making informed inventory replenishment decisions to preclude stock-outs.

- **Theoretical Underpinnings:** The ROP model serves as an algorithmic framework predicated on calculating the inventory level at which replenishment orders should be promptly initiated to obviate the potential for stock-outs during a specific lead time. It incorporates a multitude of variables including, but not limited to, lead time demand projections, safety stock allowances, and desired service levels to derive an empirically-grounded reorder point threshold. The model's incorporation of these parameters presents an amalgamated, multi-dimensional view that is amenable to customised adjustments depending on contextual nuances such as market volatility, seasonal fluctuations, and supply chain disruptions.

- **Methodological Prerequisites:** Effective deployment of the ROP model mandates an investment in robust data infrastructure. Warehouse managers, inventory strategists, and supply chain professionals must accrue precise and temporally-relevant data encompassing historical demand trends, lead time variability, and an array of supplier performance indices. Subsequent to data collection, advanced statistical methodologies—ranging from time-series analysis to probabilistic modeling—are deployed to distill this large dataset into actionable insights. The ensuing calculations yield an optimal reorder point that judiciously calibrates the trade-off between the risk of stock-outs and the financial implications of inventory carrying costs.

- **Implementation Strategies:** Implementation of the ROP model transcends mere computational exercises and entails a proactive ethos imbued within the organisational inventory management strategy. Continuous real-time surveillance of inventory positions is imperative to ensure the integrity of the pre-determined reorder point. In this vein, leveraging state-of-the-art automated inventory management systems equipped with real-time data analytics can significantly augment the precision and responsiveness of inventory management operations.

- **Multifaceted Benefits:** The utility of the ROP model transcends the rudimentary objective of averting stock-outs. Its implementation engenders a ripple effect of operational efficiencies that permeate the supply chain. By exactingly calibrating inventory levels, businesses can liberate valuable warehouse real estate for alternative utility, minimize capital immobilisation, and truncate associated carrying costs. Moreover, consistent product availability engenders heightened customer satisfaction and retention, thereby enhancing long-term brand value.

In summation, the Reorder Point (ROP) model emerges as an invaluable analytic apparatus for warehouse managers, inventory coordinators, and supply chain strategists navigating the complex domain of inventory management. It facilitates an empirically-backed equilibrium between maintaining adequate inventory levels and upholding stringent customer service standards. Through the judicious deployment of the ROP model, organisations can elevate their supply chain efficiency, achieve substantial cost savings, and amplify customer satisfaction—serving as a linchpin for overarching operational excellence in inventory management.

Just-in-Time (JIT) Inventory Management: A Multifaceted Paradigm for Operational Efficiency and Strategic Excellence

In the contemporary, hyper-competitive commercial milieu, assiduous inventory management has metamorphosed into a sine qua non for the triumphant sustainability and financial viability of organisations. Professionals such as Warehouse Managers, Inventory Managers, and practitioners of Supply Chain Management are perpetually engrossed in an intricate balancing act, aiming to calibrate their inventory levels meticulously to underpin operational efficiency and maximize the organisation's profit margins. A pivotal paradigm that has garnered extensive acclaim and adoption in modern inventory management discourses is the philosophy of Just-in-Time (JIT) Inventory Management.

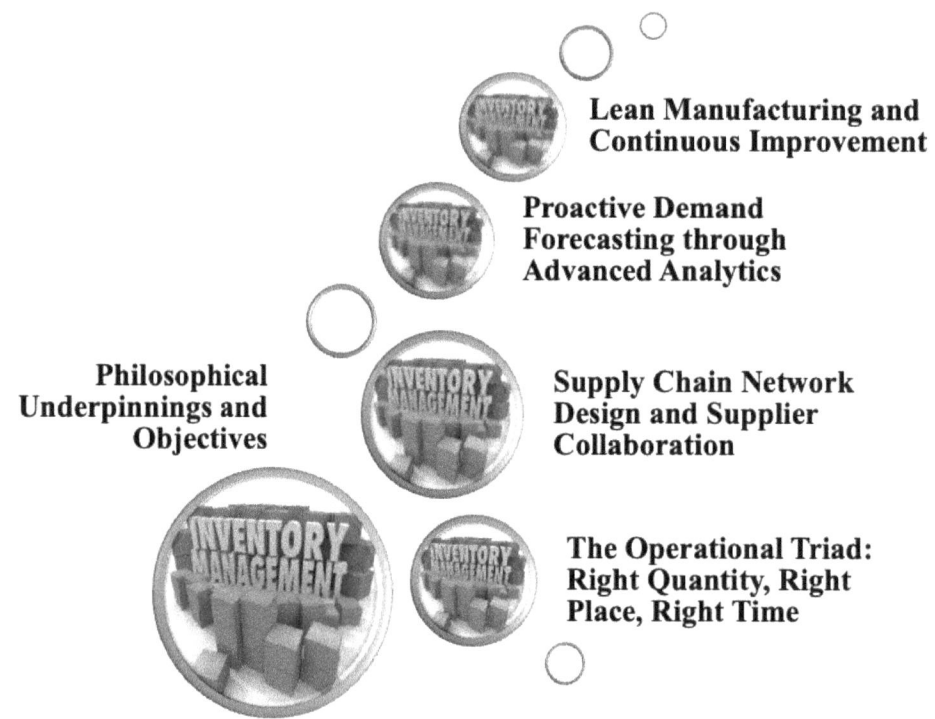

Figure 3: Just-in-Time (JIT) Inventory Management: A Multifaceted Paradigm for Operational Efficiency and Strategic Excellence

- **Philosophical Underpinnings and Objectives:** JIT Inventory Management is not merely a set of logistical procedures; rather, it represents an overarching organisational philosophy oriented towards the minimisation of waste and the attainment of operational excellence. This is achieved by orchestrating the acquisition and fabrication of goods to coincide precisely with customer demand. Distinct from more traditional inventory management methodologies, which often predicate upon the buffering of large stocks, JIT posits a radical reduction of inventory holding costs whilst striving to sustain and, often, augment levels of customer satisfaction.

- **The Operational Triad: Right Quantity, Right Place, Right Time:** The crux of JIT philosophy lies in the meticulously planned provision of the optimal quantity of inventory, situated at the appropriate locations, and made available precisely when needed. Through the assiduous minimisation of redundant inventory, the approach liberates capital otherwise immobilised in storage and mitigates the costs and risks associated with obsolescence and warehousing. The paradigm hence leans heavily on the efficacious coordination among suppliers, production facilities, and distribution channels, acting in symphony to guarantee that materials and end-products are funnelled through the supply chain with impeccable timing.

- **Supply Chain Network Design and Supplier Collaboration:** The efficacious implementation of JIT necessitates a well-architected supply chain network characterised by both responsiveness and flexibility. Warehouse Managers ought to focus assiduously on optimising operational flows, curtailing lead times, and cultivating synergistic and mutually beneficial relationships with suppliers. This supplier collaboration often extends to sharing real-time data and demand forecasts, thus facilitating a frictionless ingress of requisite materials into the production process.

- **Proactive Demand Forecasting through Advanced Analytics:** For Inventory Managers, the incorporation of JIT demands a proactive and predictive posture in demand forecasting. The application of cutting-edge analytical tools and demand forecasting algorithms enables these professionals to apprehend future customer needs and tailor inventory accretions and depletions accordingly more presciently. This heightened visibility and predictability not only curtail the incidence of stock-outs but also ameliorate on-time delivery metrics, thereby fortifying customer satisfaction indices.

- **Lean Manufacturing and Continuous Improvement:** Practitioners in the realm of Supply Chain Management are encouraged to inculcate the principles of Lean Manufacturing and Continuous Improvement as complementary methodologies that reinforce JIT objectives. Notably, Lean practices such as the employment of

Kanban systems, the execution of small-batch production cycles, and the adherence to Total Quality Management protocols, amalgamate to focus on value-added activities while extirpating inefficiencies and waste.

In summation, the Just-in-Time (JIT) Inventory Management paradigm offers a formidable toolkit enabling Warehouse Managers, Inventory Managers, and Supply Chain Management Practitioners to unlock latent efficiencies and fine-tune inventory profiles. By assimilating the tenets of JIT into their operational ethos, organisations can substantially attenuate operational costs, elevate levels of customer satisfaction, and carve out a competitive advantage in an ever-fluid business ecosystem. However, the actualisation of JIT's full potential mandates a holistic tactical framework that harmonizes supply chain optimisation, advanced forecasting methodologies, and Lean manufacturing practices. With an unwavering commitment from organisational stakeholders, the strategic deployment of JIT Inventory Management can indubitably catalyze substantial value generation, engendering long-term organisational prosperity.

ABC Analysis and Pareto Principle: Cornerstones of Strategic Inventory Management in the Supply Chain Landscape

Inventory management constitutes an indispensable facet of supply chain optimisation, meriting systematic investigation and operational acumen. Recognising the efficacy of specific managerial frameworks—such as ABC Analysis and the Pareto Principle—can substantially augment the efficiency of inventory control mechanisms. This subchapter aims to furnish an in-depth exploration of these conceptual paradigms, thereby elucidating invaluable perspectives for professionals in the fields of warehouse management, inventory control, and supply chain management.

Conceptual Underpinnings of ABC Analysis: ABC Analysis is an evaluative technique specifically contrived to segregate inventory into discrete classifications, predicated on a multidimensional evaluation of their relative importance and monetary worth. This taxonomic methodology sub-divides inventory into three distinct strata: Categories A, B, and C.

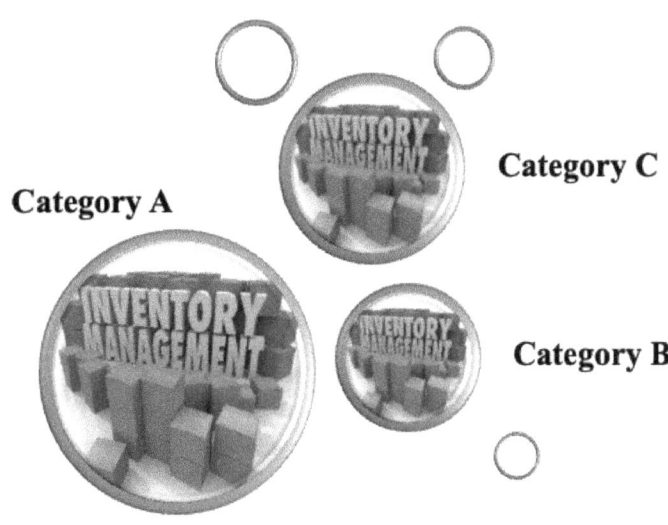

Figure 4 : Inventory into three distinct strata: Categories A, B, and C

- **Category A:** This class is emblematic of high-value items that, although occupying a minor share of the total inventory in terms of volume or quantity, command a significant percentage of the inventory's aggregate fiscal value.

- **Category B:** These items are characterised by medium value, often serving as a bridge between the high-priority Category A and the lower-priority Category C items in terms of both volume and value.
- **Category C:** This category encompasses low-value items, which despite constituting a voluminous fraction of total inventory, contribute relatively minimally to the overall monetary value of the stock.

By judiciously executing an ABC Analysis, warehouse and inventory managers are empowered to stratify their managerial focus and resource allocation protocols. Items classified under Category A, owing to their high intrinsic value and operational criticality, warrant meticulous oversight and rigorous inventory control measures to obviate stockouts and preserve product availability. Conversely, Category C items, given their nominal value, can be managed with a lenient oversight regime, thereby facilitating managerial focus on high-priority areas and attenuating operational expenditures.

Symbiotic Relationship between ABC Analysis and the Pareto Principle: The Pareto Principle, colloquially known as the 80/20 rule, maintains a symbiotic theoretical rapport with ABC Analysis. This heuristic posits that a disproportionately large percentage of effects—approximately 80%—emanate from a relatively sparse set of causes—around 20%. In the realm of inventory management, this translates to the assertion that nearly 80% of an organisation's revenue or sales volume is typically attributable to a mere 20% of the stocked items. By ascertaining these 'vital few,' managers are strategically positioned to concentrate on optimising inventory practices and supply chain processes pertinent to these crucial items.

Synchronising the application of the Pareto Principle with ABC Analysis equips managers with the analytical acumen to tailor distinct strategies for each category. For instance, Category A items could warrant capital investment in cutting-edge forecasting algorithms and granular demand planning methodologies to mitigate the risk of stockouts and buttress customer satisfaction metrics. In contrast, Category C items might be more amenable to cost-saving strategies like bulk procurement or vendor-managed inventory agreements, which can engender operational fluidity while concurrently reducing carrying costs.

Consequential Benefits of Integrated Application: Adoption and coherent implementation of ABC Analysis in conjunction with the Pareto Principle yield manifold dividends in the realm of inventory management. These benefits range from efficacious resource allocation to the diminution of carrying costs, optimal calibration of order quantities, and enhancement of customer service quality levels. Equipped with a nuanced understanding of the intrinsic value and operational import of each inventory item, professionals in warehouse management, inventory control, and supply chain management are well-poised to actualize operational efficiencies and achieve strategic objectives.

In summation, ABC Analysis and the Pareto Principle stand as instrumental paradigms for inventory management. These frameworks empower warehouse managers, inventory control specialists, and supply chain management practitioners to strategically categorize inventory items based on multidimensional metrics of value and significance. By focusing managerial attention and resources on the 'vital few,' these professionals can optimize supply chain processes, thereby engendering substantial cost savings and bolstering customer satisfaction. In an era where efficient supply chain operations are critical for competitive advantage, the comprehension and application of these methodologies are indispensable.

5. CHAPTER 5: INVENTORY VISIBILITY AND TRACKING

Utilizing Technology for Real-time Inventory Visibility: A Critical Discourse

In the contemporary, rapidly evolving business milieu, efficacious inventory management emerges as a sine qua non for the organizational prosperity and operational excellence. Practitioners occupying various echelons in warehouse management, inventory stewardship, and supply chain management are confronted with the Herculean task of ensuring precise and real-time insight into inventory metrics. This subchapter delineates the salient features and transformative potential of technological advancements in engendering enhanced inventory management, thereby facilitating strategic efficacy in supply chain operations.

- **Paradigm Shifts Enabled by Technological Innovations:** The landscape of business operations has been irrevocably altered by technological advancements, with inventory management representing a quintessential domain experiencing such a metamorphosis. The advent of sophisticated, high-caliber inventory management systems has endowed warehouse managers with the capability to maintain real-time, panoramic visibility over inventory metrics throughout the entire concatenation of the supply chain. This unobstructed visibility serves as a linchpin for data-driven decision-making processes, aids in the optimisation of inventory storage parameters, and fosters an agile response mechanism to vicissitudes in market demand.

- **Technological Catalysts: Barcode and RFID Technologies:** One of the seminal technologies engendering real-time inventory visibility is the symbiotic integration of barcode and Radio Frequency Identification (RFID) technologies. Through the employment of either barcode or RFID tags appended to individual merchandise, managers can assiduously track the merchandise's trajectory from its ingress into the warehouse milieu to its ultimate shipment to the consumer. This capability for real-time tracking augments the fidelity of inventory audits, ameliorates the risks associated with stock deficiencies or surplus, and obviates the necessity for labor-intensive manual data entry.

- **The Augmentation through Advanced Inventory Management Software:** Subsequent to the technological augmentation is the incorporation of advanced inventory management software applications that arm warehouse managers with an extensive repertoire of tools for inventory data surveillance, tracking, and analytical assessment. Through real-time dashboards and exhaustive reporting mechanisms, these software solutions confer invaluable insights into inventory status, demand fluctuation patterns, and supplier efficacy metrics. Such insights empower managers to fine-tune inventory holding expenditures, streamline the machinations of order fulfilment, and elevate the overall levels of customer satisfaction.

- **Interoperability and System Integration:** Moreover, the seamless interoperability of these technological solutions with other pivotal supply chain management software frameworks—such as Enterprise Resource Planning (ERP) or Customer Relationship Management (CRM) systems—serves to further fortify real-time inventory visibility. The synergistic linkage of these disparate systems enables a holistic and temporally up-to-date view of inventory data across multifarious organisational departments and geographical locales. This integrative facility significantly elevates the level of intra-organisational coordination and judicious decision-making.

In summation, the technological revolution in facilitating real-time inventory visibility stands as a veritable game-changer for practitioners in warehouse management, inventory stewardship, and the broader field of supply chain management. By harnessing the transformative power of barcode and RFID technologies, avant-garde inventory management software, and system integration strategies, these professionals can manifest remarkable efficiencies, trim operational costs, and achieve unparalleled advancements in overarching supply chain performance matrices. Embracing this pantheon of technological innovations is not merely an advantageous strategy in today's intensely competitive business topography but also a prerequisite for maintaining a vanguard position in the perpetually evolving domain of inventory management.

Barcode and RFID Technology: Pioneering Efficiency in Inventory Management

In the relentless, fast-paced arena of inventory management, the imperative to meticulously track products and fortify the supply chain efficacy is paramount. Enter the transformative capabilities of barcode and RFID technologies, which have drastically revolutionised the modus operandi of warehouses and instantiated unparalleled levels of efficiency.

- **The Indelible Impact of Barcode Technology:** Initially conceived and widely deployed for decades, barcode technology employs a cryptic encoding of information within a sequence of parallel lines that serve as a unique ontological identifier for each SKU (Stock Keeping Unit). Scanning these barcodes—either via handheld devices or static scanning stations deployed at critical junctions in the supply chain, such as receiving docks, picking aisles, and shipping areas—facilitates real-time inventory tracking, attenuates the incidence of data-entry errors, and furnishes accurate metrics that serve as the substrate for informed decision-making.

- **Salient Benefits of Barcode Technology:** The dividends reaped from barcode technology are multifold. Firstly, its capability for expedited and accurate data capture minimizes the propensity for human-induced data entry anomalies, thus amplifying productivity and engendering increased operational efficiency. Secondly, barcodes are readily amenable to facile integration with other extant systems, notably Warehouse Management Systems (WMS) and Enterprise Resource Planning (ERP) frameworks. This confluence engenders a seamless real-time visibility into inventory parameters, lubricates the gears of order fulfilment procedures, and enables the generation of more accurate and predictive demand forecasting algorithms.

- **RFID: The Next Frontier:** Transcending the capabilities of traditional barcodes, Radio Frequency Identification (RFID) technology leverages microchips and antennas to wirelessly transmit intricate information to RFID readers. A salient advantage of RFID technology is that it obviates the need for line-of-sight scanning and permits remote scanning capabilities, even when the tags are obscured within product packaging or are enmeshed in a cluster of products.

- **Profound Advantages of RFID Technology:** The benefits accruing from RFID technology are substantial and far-reaching. Firstly, it enables the concomitant scanning of a multitude of items, expediting the inventory audit process and attenuating labor expenditures. Secondly, the voluminous data storage capabilities of RFID tags allow for granular tracking of item attributes, shelf-life parameters, and historical locational data. This granularity renders invaluable insights into the dynamics of inventory performance and proves instrumental in diagnosing systemic bottlenecks or potential areas necessitating strategic intervention within the supply chain.

In summation, the roles of warehouse managers, inventory managers, and supply chain management professionals are greatly augmented by the prudent implementation of barcode and RFID technologies. The incorporation of these technologies represents an essential stratagem for streamlining operations, mitigating costs, and enhancing customer satisfaction metrics. Remaining au courant with the ceaseless advancements in these technological platforms is not merely advisable but imperative for maintaining a competitive edge in the ever-fluctuating landscape of inventory management.

Warehouse Management Systems (WMS): A Locus of Technological Transformation in Modern Inventory Management Paradigms

In the contemporary landscape of ceaselessly competitive and dynamically evolving business ecosystems, effective and efficient management of warehousing operations emerges as a sine qua non for organisational viability and success. As custodians of this critical function, warehouse managers, inventory overseers, and supply chain management experts are mandated to judiciously employ both strategic frameworks and tactical tools to augment and streamline their inventory management practices. Within this context, the advent of Warehouse Management Systems (WMS) serves as a disruptive technological innovation that has fundamentally redefined traditional paradigms of inventory management. This subchapter aims to explicate the intricate features and multifarious benefits of WMS technologies, elucidating how their deployment can serve as a catalyst for operational efficiency in inventory management.

- **Inventory Tracking and Control: The Pillars of Real-Time Visibility:** One of the most salient functionalities offered by Warehouse Management Systems is the systematisation of inventory tracking and control mechanisms. Utilising state-of-the-art technologies such as barcode scanning and Radio-Frequency Identification (RFID), WMS systems afford managers a level of real-time visibility heretofore unattainable through conventional methodologies. This constant awareness allows for accurate inventory quantification and surveillance, ensuring the temporal and spatial availability of products. Consequently, this minimizes detrimental stockout conditions while simultaneously preventing the financial drain associated with overstock scenarios. Furthermore, WMS systems furnish granular analytics pertaining to inventory turnover ratios, thereby enabling managerial staff to pinpoint slow-moving items and implement nuanced strategies aimed at optimising stock levels.

- **Order Fulfilment Optimisation: Orchestrating Efficiency through Automation:** A second indispensable feature of WMS platforms is the automation of order processing and picking procedures, thereby engendering marked reductions in human errors and substantially augmenting order accuracy. By employing algorithmic calculations, Warehouse Management Systems empower managers to allocate human and material resources judiciously, optimize picking pathways within the warehouse, and prioritise orders contingent upon customer specifications and exigencies. The resultant operational landscape is one characterised by expedited order fulfilment cycles, elevated customer satisfaction indices, and a significant contraction in operational expenditures.

- **Advanced Analytics and Reporting: Empowering Decision-Making through Data:** In an era where data-driven decisions are increasingly considered the cornerstone of effective management, WMS technologies further distinguish themselves through their provision of advanced analytics and reporting functionalities. Warehouse managers can generate real-time, actionable reports delineated by key performance indicators (KPIs), such as order accuracy rates, on-time delivery percentages, and inventory turnover frequencies. These analytics not only facilitate the identification of operational bottlenecks but also provide a quantifiable measure of the efficacy of existing inventory management strategies, thereby allowing for continual refinements and adjustments.

In summation, Warehouse Management Systems (WMS) constitute an instrumental asset for warehouse managers, inventory coordinators, and supply chain management professionals. These technological solutions serve to instantiate real-time visibility into inventory metrics, automate complex operational workflows, and provide a rich analytical framework for data-driven decision-making. By integrating a WMS into their operational infrastructure, organisations can efficaciously enhance their inventory management protocols, engender cost efficiencies, and ameliorate overall warehouse performance metrics. As such, the strategic implementation of a WMS system emerges not merely as a desirable adjunct, but as an indispensable component for any enterprise aiming to fortify its supply chain and attain a sustainable competitive advantage in the increasingly complex milieu of inventory management.

Optimal Inventory Tracking Protocols in Contemporary Business Environments

In the contemporary commercial milieu characterised by an unparalleled dynamism and a relentless competitive fervor, efficacious inventory management serves as an indispensable cornerstone for organisational operational excellence and customer contentment. This subsection aims to delve deeply into the cardinal best practices that pertain to inventory tracking. The purpose is to illuminate a comprehensive understanding that would be invaluable to professionals such as warehouse managers, inventory administrators, and experts in the realm of supply chain management, particularly those specialising in inventory governance.

- **Integration of Sophisticated Inventory Monitoring Infrastructures:** In a data-driven, hyper-connected world, the imperative to invest in cutting-edge inventory tracking technologies cannot be overemphasised. Advanced systems, deploying emergent technologies like barcode scanning, Radio-Frequency Identification (RFID), and real-time data analytics, facilitate an instantaneous and unambiguous visibility into the movements and statuses of inventories. By embracing these advanced tracking systems, warehouse managers not only ameliorate the risks associated with manual data entry inaccuracies but also significantly expedite the process of order fulfilment. Moreover, these technologies serve as pivotal enablers in the optimisation of inventory replenishment algorithms, thereby contributing to overall supply chain efficiency.

- **Institutionalisation of Periodic Cycle Counting Protocols:** Cycle counting represents an established practice that entails the periodic execution of physical inventory counts. The intent is to establish an unerring baseline of inventory accuracy and to precipitously identify any incongruities or discrepancies. The adoption of a rigorously structured cycle counting regimen equips warehouse managers with the capabilities to maintain punctiliously accurate inventory records, thereby mitigating the risks of either stock-outs or overstocks. Additionally, recurrent cycle counting serves as an invaluable diagnostic tool to flag any latent inefficiencies in inventory processes or supply chain operations, paving the way for iterative improvements in overarching inventory accuracy.

- **Implementation of ABC Inventory Stratification Methodology:** ABC analysis operates on the principle of categorising inventory items according to their financial impact and strategic importance to the business operation. Inventory items are taxonomically classified into A, B, and C categories, which enable warehouse managers to prioritize focus and resource allocation effectively. Items classified as 'A' typically constitute a minority of total inventory but represent a disproportionately high financial value; hence, they warrant scrupulous attention and management. 'B' items embody moderate value and importance, while 'C' items, often representing the majority of stock-keeping units (SKUs), require less rigorous monitoring and management due to their relatively minimal financial impact.

- **Formulation of Data-Driven Reorder Point Thresholds:** Ascertaining precise reorder points is of paramount importance for precluding undesirable outcomes such as stock-outs or bloated inventory levels. The calibration of reorder points should be grounded in a comprehensive analysis that incorporates variables such as demand patterns, lead times, and targeted service levels. By operationalising data-driven reorder thresholds, organisations can judiciously maintain adequate stock levels, curtail holding expenditures, and guarantee the prompt fulfilment of customer orders.

- **Incorporation of Prognostic Demand Forecasting Mechanisms:** Accurate demand forecasting is a critical determinant in the optimisation of inventory tracking. Managers should exploit a melange of historical data, emergent market trends, and nuanced customer behavior analytics to generate dependable demand forecasts. Such predictive insights capacitate proactive inventory strategising, which in turn minimizes the risk of stock-outs and excess inventory, ultimately optimising resource allocation and operational efficiency.

- **Cultivation of Collaborative Synergies and Transparent Communication Channels:** Effective inventory management is an inherently collaborative endeavour that necessitates the synchronous engagement of diverse stakeholders such as suppliers, manufacturers, and distributors. It is incumbent upon warehouse managers to instate explicit and unambiguous channels of communication, ensuring regular exchanges of pertinent information. This fosters accurate demand forecasting, timely order placement, and ultimately engenders a seamlessly integrated inventory management ecosystem.

In summary, the assiduous application of these preeminent best practices in inventory tracking will equip warehouse managers, inventory coordinators, and supply chain specialists with the requisite toolkit to augment operational efficiency, streamline intricate processes, and elevate customer satisfaction indices. The cornerstone for achieving this lies in the judicious integration of advanced technological solutions, the institutionalisation of empirically validated processes, and the nurturing of collaborative relationships among key stakeholders. Collectively, these strategic elements coalesce to form a robust framework for optimised inventory management, thus paving the way for sustainable organisational success in an ever-competitive marketplace.

6. CHAPTER 6: INVENTORY ACCURACY AND CYCLE COUNTING

Cycle Counting Methodology: A Multifaceted Approach to Inventory Accuracy and Operational Efficiency

In the intricate domain of inventory management, the confluence of accuracy and efficiency assumes critical importance. Ensuring the unerring operation of warehouse activities is not merely an operational need but a strategic imperative. One instrumental methodology designed to accomplish this objective is cycle counting. This subchapter aims to elucidate the various dimensions of cycle counting methodology in a thorough manner. The discussion is geared towards providing indispensable insights to warehouse managers, inventory control specialists, and professionals engaged in the broader sphere of supply chain management.

The Imperative of Cycle Counting Methodology

Cycle counting represents a systematic, iterative procedure aimed at substantiating the veracity of inventory records by conducting frequent but partial counts of stock items. This stands in contrast to traditional full-scale physical inventories, which are not only labor-intensive but also intrusive to ongoing operations. Cycle counting offers a methodology for perpetual verification, thus eliminating workflow disruptions. Through the consistent counting of segmented portions of inventory, discrepancies between recorded and actual stocks can be quickly identified and rectified. This leads to a cascade of benefits including increased inventory accuracy, reduced instances of inventory shrinkage, and heightened levels of customer satisfaction.

Advantages of Implementing Cycle Counting Methodology

Adoption of cycle counting methodology engenders numerous advantages. Chief among these is the obviation of the need for comprehensive, wall-to-wall inventory counts, thus economising both time and organisational resources. Moreover, the fidelity of inventory records attained through cycle counting enables more astute decision-making processes. This, in turn, optimizes order fulfilment metrics and minimizes the occurrence of stock-outs, thereby directly influencing revenue generation. Furthermore, cycle counting serves as a diagnostic tool to reveal latent inefficiencies in inventory processes and contributes to root cause analyses, thereby fostering a culture of continuous improvement in inventory management paradigms.

Taxonomy of Cycle Counting Methodologies

Within the umbrella term of cycle counting, there exists a plurality of specialised methodologies. A noteworthy technique is the ABC analysis, wherein items are categorised based on their economic significance and operational criticality. This classification serves as the basis for prioritising which items are subjected to more frequent counts. Additionally, the frequency of cycle counts can be tailored according to specific metrics such as item turnover rates, fiscal value, and historical accuracy levels, allowing for a nuanced approach to inventory verification.

Best Practices in Conducting Cycle Counts

Executional precision is paramount in cycle counting. This section delineates the optimal practices for data acquisition, including the employment of technological aids such as barcode scanners and dedicated inventory management software systems. Equally salient is the need for specialised training programs aimed at warehouse personnel. These programs are designed to ensure proficiency in accurate counting techniques and in the expeditious resolution of discrepancies, thereby reinforcing the integrity of the cycle counting process.

Data Analysis and Reporting Mechanisms

The utility of cycle counting is not confined to the act of counting alone. In fact, the subsequent data analysis and reporting processes are pivotal in unlocking its full potential. By scrutinising the collated data for trends and anomalies, cycle counting serves as a catalyst for proactive inventory management strategies. Furthermore, well-designed reporting systems function as early warning mechanisms, swiftly flagging discrepancies and averting the adverse repercussions of stock-outs or overstock situations.

In sum, the mastery of cycle counting methodology constitutes an invaluable asset in the arsenal of inventory management strategies. Through its strategic implementation, organisations can realize a panoply of benefits including heightened operational efficiency, cost reductions, and elevated levels of customer satisfaction. Thus, this subchapter endeavours to serve as an exhaustive and insightful guide for stakeholders engaged in warehouse management, inventory control, and the wider realm of supply chain management, advocating for the optimisation of inventory management practices through the systematic implementation of cycle counting.

Inventory Discrepancy Resolution: An Indispensable Component of Strategic Inventory Management

In the high-stakes, rapidly evolving milieu of supply chain management, inventory discrepancies represent a formidable obstacle that can undermine operational efficiency, inflate expenditure, and detract from customer satisfaction. Consequently, it becomes imperative for professionals engrossed in inventory management to comprehend the salient importance of inventory discrepancy resolution. Effective strategies must be conceived and executed to rectify such discrepancies expeditiously.

Conceptualising Inventory Discrepancy

Inventory discrepancy is construed as the discordance between the empirically assessed physical stock count and the digitised, system-recorded inventory levels. Such incongruences may materialize owing to a multitude of causative factors, encompassing theft, procedural errors in receiving or picking merchandise, degradation of physical goods, or data entry inaccuracies. Independent of the genesis, the prompt resolution of these discrepancies is pivotal for ensuring inventory integrity, unobstructed operational flow, and the preservation of customer goodwill.

Methodological Approach for Resolution

The inaugural step in combating inventory discrepancies is the systematic execution of routine physical stock counts, alternatively known as cycle counts. This comparative analysis between the tactile count and the archival inventory data serves a dual purpose: it identifies extant discrepancies and facilitates the process of delving into the underlying root causes. Once these are elucidated, a panoply of corrective actions can be instituted to ameliorate the situation.

Standardised Procedures and Technological Interventions

An efficacious strategy for the resolution of inventory discrepancies hinges on the formulation and rigorous enforcement of standardized protocols for receiving, picking, and the holistic management of inventory. Implementation of cutting-edge identification technologies, such as barcode or RFID (Radio Frequency Identification) scanning, can substantially attenuate the incidence of human errors in data transcription. Moreover, comprehensive training modules designed for warehouse personnel can assuage discrepancies emanating from negligence or informational voids.

Investigative Measures

Upon the detection of discrepancies, a meticulous investigation is warranted to ascertain the root cause. Procedures may encompass the scrutiny of CCTV (Closed-Circuit Television) surveillance footage, the solicitation of testimonials from staff, and the commencement of rigorous internal audits. The revelation of the causative agent allows for the implementation of targeted interventions designed to forestall the reoccurrence of analogous irregularities in future operational cycles.

Supplier and Customer Communication

The linchpin of effective inventory discrepancy resolution resides in the maintenance of transparent communication channels with both suppliers and clientele. Prompt dissemination of information relating to stock discrepancies expedites the resolution process and mitigates the potential for logistical complications within the supply chain. Collaborative engagements with stakeholders can further lubricate the exchange of pertinent information, thereby elevating the fidelity of inventory records.

Continuous Improvement in Inventory Accuracy: The Bedrock of Supply Chain Excellence

The imperative for unimpeachable inventory accuracy permeates all echelons of supply chain management. A lapse in this crucial aspect can engender a cascade of operational setbacks, ranging from stockouts and surplus inventory to escalating carrying costs, declining customer satisfaction, and the ultimate forfeiture of revenue streams. This necessitates a relentless focus on the continuous amelioration of inventory accuracy as a strategic priority for warehouse managers, inventory managers, and practitioners in the supply chain domain.

Strategies for Ongoing Refinement

This subchapter elucidates an array of tactical interventions and industry best practices designed to engender a culture of perpetual improvement in inventory accuracy. Paramount among these is the establishment of a robust inventory management infrastructure, buttressed by avant-garde technological solutions and impeccable data capture methodologies. Investments in automated inventory tracking architectures, such as barcode or RFID systems, yield dividends in the form of heightened accuracy and procedural efficiency.

Routine Inventory Reconciliation

Regularised physical inventory counts and subsequent reconciliations are pivotal for maintaining accuracy. Implementation of cycle counting, a nuanced approach to periodic item-level stock verification, enhances both the fidelity and timeliness of inventory records while concurrently minimising operational disruptions.

Communication and Role Accountability

Interdepartmental communication assumes critical importance in the pursuit of inventory accuracy. Regular briefing sessions and open lines of communication enable cross-functional collaboration, fostering a shared understanding of potential challenges and facilitating the execution of remedial measures. Clearly delineated roles and responsibilities within the inventory management ecosystem ensure alignment and coordinated action toward common objectives.

Data Analytics and Decision Support Systems

The subchapter also delves into the manifold advantages of employing advanced data analytics and reporting mechanisms in inventory management. Leveraging sophisticated analytical tools enables decision-makers to glean actionable insights into inventory dynamics, demand fluctuation patterns, and predictive forecasting accuracy. These insights inform strategic choices, optimize inventory holdings, and diminish the likelihood of resource wastage through stock-outs or excess inventory scenarios.

In summation, the quest for continuous improvement in inventory accuracy is not a finite endeavour but rather an ongoing commitment requiring institutionalised excellence and a culture oriented toward ceaseless learning and refinement. By deploying the strategies and best practices elucidated herein, stakeholders in the supply chain can optimize inventory management protocols, curtail operational expenditures, amplify customer satisfaction metrics, and unlock unparalleled efficiencies in supply chain processes.

Importance of Inventory Accuracy

Inventory accuracy, an essential aspect of supply chain optimization, stands as a cardinal component that shapes the efficacy of warehouse operations. This subsection aims to shed light on the pivotal role of inventory accuracy and its ensuing implications for an array of stakeholders, including warehouse managers, inventory managers, and practitioners in the field of supply chain management.

The concept of inventory accuracy pertains to the exactitude and fidelity of inventory records in relation to the actual, tangible stock situated within a warehouse environment. It is imperative that numerical entries concerning inventory are congruent with the physical inventory to ensure the integrity of data-driven decision-making processes. Multiple facets of business operations stand to gain from heightened levels of inventory accuracy for several compelling reasons.

First and foremost, inventory accuracy serves as a cornerstone for customer satisfaction. Precise and dependable inventory records empower warehouse managers to assiduously fulfil customer orders, thereby obviating the possibilities of stock-outs or inordinate delays. Such an endeavour begets enhanced customer service metrics and amplifies the overall consumer experience. In stark contrast, inventories marked by imprecisions can instigate an array of customer dissatisfaction outcomes, such as order cancellations, protracted backorders, and erroneous shipments, all of which can engender not only immediate revenue loss but also inflict long-term reputational damage.

Secondarily, the attainment of scrupulous inventory management galvanizes the optimisation of warehouse operations. A warehouse endowed with reliable inventory data is poised to enact judicious decisions in the arenas of stock replenishment, spatial allocation for storage, and the efficient execution of order picking. Such prudent measures deter instances of overstocking and under-stocking, curtail superfluous inventory carrying costs, and diminish the likelihood of obsolescence or spoilage of items. Furthermore, accurate inventory metrics facilitate expeditious order fulfilment procedures, thereby truncating order cycle times and amplifying the overall throughput of warehouse operations.

Inventory managers, too, are beneficiaries of high-fidelity inventory data, which serves as an indispensable asset for demand forecasting and strategic inventory planning. By assiduously scrutinising historical sales data juxtaposed against extant inventory levels, inventory managers can discern emerging trends, fine-tune demand forecasts, and judiciously modulate stock levels. This orchestration aids in mitigating the pitfalls associated with excess inventory, thereby diminishing holding costs and enhancing liquidity metrics.

Supply chain management experts derive distinct advantages from an architecture grounded in accurate inventory management. Such practitioners exploit precise inventory data as a cornerstone to render informed, strategic resolutions concerning sourcing paradigms, logistics, and distribution channels. The availability of reliable inventory information enables the identification of latent bottlenecks or inefficiencies within the supply chain, thereby providing the impetus for the timely initiation of corrective actions. The ensuing outcome is an elevated state of supply chain visibility, truncated lead times, and an overarching improvement in the performance metrics of the supply chain.

In summation, the veracity of inventory data occupies a central role in shaping the success trajectories of warehouse managers, inventory managers, and experts in the domain of supply chain management. The precision of inventory records engenders an array of salutary outcomes, ranging from the amplification of customer satisfaction metrics and operational efficiencies to fostering informed decision-making in both inventory planning and supply chain management. By internalising the imperative of inventory accuracy and adopting robust inventory governance protocols, organisations can catalyse operational efficiencies, drive cost reductions, and secure a competitive advantage in an increasingly volatile business landscape.

7. CHAPTER 7: SUPPLY CHAIN COLLABORATION AND VENDOR MANAGED INVENTORY (VMI)

Collaborative Relationships with Suppliers: A Bedrock for Optimising Inventory Management in a Volatile Market Environment

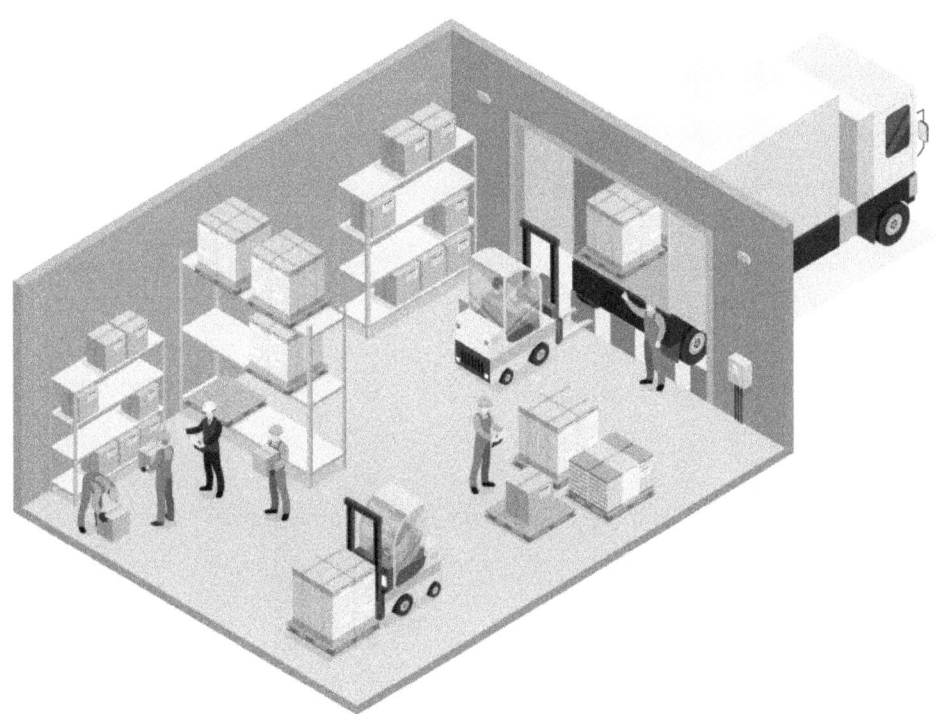

In the complex and perpetually fluid landscape of supply chain management, the quintessential role of nurturing collaborative relationships with suppliers is irrefutably indispensable. Those entrusted with warehouse management, inventory oversight, and the broader responsibilities of supply chain orchestration are acutely aware of the pivotal function that judicious inventory management serves in augmenting operational efficiency and actualising the overarching strategic goals of the organisation.

The Indispensable Role of Suppliers in Inventory Management

When contemplating the multifaceted sphere of inventory management, it becomes readily apparent that suppliers serve as an essential lynchpin in safeguarding the unobstructed and efficient flow of goods and materials across the continuum of the supply chain. Through the initiation and ongoing cultivation of synergistic relationships with suppliers, warehouse managers and inventory control experts can actualize an array of consequential benefits, which have a direct and amplifying impact on inventory management efficacy.

Facilitating Open Communication and Transparent Information Sharing

Primarily, an ingrained culture of collaboration with suppliers serves as a conduit for open lines of communication and transparent information exchange. This facilitative environment engenders warehouse managers with unparalleled access to salient data concerning supplier competencies, lead time variability, and looming potential disruptions in the supply chain ecosystem. Empowered with precise and punctiliously-timed information, inventory managers can make data-driven determinations that allow for the strategic planning of inventory levels. This, in turn, enables them to calibrate safety stock thresholds judiciously, attenuate the incidence of stockouts, and obviate superfluous inventory holdings, thereby enhancing customer satisfaction while concurrently diminishing carrying costs.

Cultivating Trust and Mutual Understanding for Win-Win Outcomes

Beyond the mere transactional aspects, fostering robust collaborative partnerships with suppliers engenders a climate of mutual trust and shared understanding. Within this relational paradigm, warehouse managers are better positioned to engage in constructive negotiations aimed at securing favorable contractual terms. Such terms may encompass competitive pricing structures, adaptively flexible delivery timetables, and incremental improvements in product quality metrics. By maintaining close operational alignment with suppliers, inventory management professionals can identify and act upon opportunities for collaborative ventures geared towards process optimisation. These could involve the adoption of lean inventory methodologies, or the implementation of just-in-time inventory replenishment paradigms. Collective endeavours of this ilk can precipitate substantive cost-efficiencies, enhance product availability, and promote a more streamlined, responsive inventory management apparatus.

Leveraging Supplier Expertise for Strategic Advantage

Furthermore, the symbiotic relationships cultivated with suppliers offer warehouse managers the opportunity to tap into an invaluable reservoir of sector-specific expertise and market acumen. Suppliers can proffer keen insights into macro-level market trends, impending new product rollouts, and nascent technological innovations. By harnessing this wealth of knowledge, practitioners in the domain of supply chain management can make anticipatory, strategically-astute decisions that facilitate the optimal alignment of product assortments. This enables them to seize emerging market opportunities with alacrity and thus not only amplifies inventory management practices but also augments the organisation's competitive resilience.

In summation, the multitudinous advantages conferred by the cultivation of collaborative relationships with suppliers are incontrovertible, particularly within the specialized ambit of inventory management. Warehouse managers, inventory coordinators, and supply chain management strategists must, therefore, accord due recognition to the cardinal importance of initiating and assiduously nurturing these symbiotic partnerships. By anchoring their practices in the principles of open communication, trust, and mutual beneficence, they can effectively leverage supplier capabilities, refine operational processes, and thereby fulfill their inventory management objectives in an increasingly unpredictable market environment.

Vendor Managed Inventory: A Scholarly Exploration of its Benefits and Challenges

Vendor Managed Inventory (VMI) serves as an innovative paradigm shift within the realm of inventory management, adopting a collaborative schema where the vendor assumes the onus for maintaining optimal inventory levels at the client's storage facility or distribution center. This subchapter undertakes a nuanced dissection of the manifold advantages and potential obstacles concomitant with the deployment of Vendor Managed Inventory systems within the broader scope of supply chain management.

Advantages of Vendor Managed Inventory

- **Augmented Operational Efficiency:** The VMI paradigm offers a potent avenue for engendering efficiency within the supply chain by mitigating stockout instances and excess inventory scenarios. Through delegating the inventory monitoring and adjustment responsibilities to vendors, warehouse managers are liberated to allocate their cognitive and operational resources towards other mission-critical functions, culminating in an elevation of overall organisational efficiency.
- **Cost Efficacy:** The VMI approach is instrumental in attenuating the financial burden associated with inventory carrying costs. By situating the responsibility of maintaining optimal stock levels squarely on the vendor, the

requisites for safety stock are rendered moot, thus obviating the fiscal risks associated with obsolescence and contributing to substantial cost savings.

- **Strengthened Inter-Organisational Collaboration:** VMI fosters an environment conducive to collaborative endeavours between vendors and clients. The mutual exchange of real-time data pertaining to inventory levels, demand trends, and lead times cultivates a data-driven decision-making ethos. This reciprocative symbiosis can engender more precise demand forecasting and refined inventory planning protocols.

- **Enhancement of Customer Satisfaction:** VMI enables warehouse managers to guarantee the expeditious availability of products, thereby curtailing stockouts and amplifying customer satisfaction metrics. Vendors can adaptively calibrate inventory levels in response to demand fluctuations, ensuring an unerring provision of the appropriate products.

Challenges of Vendor Managed Inventory

- **Integration and Data Sharing Complexities:** The successful integration of VMI mandates a seamless amalgamation of information systems and the unobstructed flow of real-time data between the participating entities. This is especially arduous when interfacing with a multiplicity of vendors utilizing divergent technological platforms.

- **Issues Pertaining to Trust and Communication:** The VMI model is predicated on the cornerstone of trust and transparent communication channels between the involved parties. The inception and maintenance of such collaborative rapport can be encumbered by opaque operational strategies or conflicting organizational objectives.

- **Increased Vendor Dependence:** A byproduct of the VMI system is the heightened reliance of warehouse managers on vendor efficacy in inventory management. This symbiotic dependence engenders vulnerabilities, particularly in scenarios where the vendor is remiss in meeting performance benchmarks or encounters disruptions in their supply chain logistics.

- **Implementation Complexities:** The instantiation of a VMI system necessitates meticulous planning, workflow reengineering, and change management oversight. This typically involves substantial preliminary capital outlays in technological infrastructure, in addition to the education and training requisites for warehouse and inventory management personnel.

Vendor Managed Inventory offers a compendium of benefits such as operational efficiency augmentation, cost reduction, collaboration enhancement, and customer satisfaction improvement. However, it concomitantly introduces complexities related to data integration, trust cultivation, dependency management, and implementation logistics. Thus, it becomes imperative for warehouse managers, inventory specialists, and supply chain management experts to scrupulously appraise these dynamics prior to committing to a VMI-based inventory management methodology.

Implementing Vendor Managed Inventory Programs: A Comprehensive Guide

In an era characterised by relentless market dynamism and intense competitive pressures, efficacious inventory management emerges as an indispensable linchpin for organisational longevity and prosperity. Vendor Managed Inventory (VMI), an increasingly pervasive strategy in this landscape, presents myriad opportunities and challenges for key stakeholders in the supply chain. This subchapter elucidates the procedural intricacies and ensuing benefits of implementing VMI initiatives.

Implementation Guidelines and Stakeholder Roles

The successful operationalisation of VMI programs demands an intricate choreography involving multiple stakeholders.

- **Role of Warehouse Managers:** These professionals bear the responsibility for engendering the infrastructural and systemic preconditions requisite for VMI. This frequently necessitates capital investment in state-of-the-art technologies that facilitate real-time inventory surveillance and inter-organisational communication conduits.

- **Role of Inventory Managers:** These stakeholders are tasked with acquiring an intimate comprehension of their inventory needs and transmitting this information cogently to vendors. Additionally, they are accountable for formulating key performance indicators (KPIs) to evaluate the efficacy of the VMI engagement. Typical KPIs might encompass metrics such as stockout rate reduction, order fulfilment rate augmentation, and carrying cost minimisation.

Benefits for Supply Chain Management Practitioners

- **Collaborative Synergy and Cost-Optimisation:** VMI programs are quintessentially collaborative, engendering robust inter-organisational relationships that yield tangible dividends. Synergistic partnerships facilitate the identification and execution of process improvements and cost rationalisation strategies.

- **Strategic Focus:** The transference of replenishment responsibilities to the vendor liberates supply chain managers to allocate resources towards strategic functions. This includes nuanced analysis of demand proclivities, long-term forecasting, and the design of supply chain optimisation strategies.

The implementation of Vendor Managed Inventory programs affords a plethora of advantages to various supply chain constituents, ranging from warehouse managers to supply chain strategists. These benefits encompass collaborative enrichment, cost mitigation, and an elevated operational efficiency. As such, VMI serves as a potent mechanism for deriving competitive advantage in an increasingly complex and volatile business milieu.

Continuous Improvement as a Cornerstone of Operational Excellence in Vendor Managed Inventory (VMI) Processes

In the dynamically shifting landscape of supply chain management, the paradigm of continuous improvement has ascended as an indispensable enabler for attaining a pinnacle of operational excellence. This premise is markedly applicable in the realm of inventory management, a function of quintessential import within an organisation's overarching supply chain systematics. The focus of this subchapter is to delve into the crucial role of continuous improvement in Vendor Managed Inventory (VMI) processes and to explicate how such a commitment can serve as a linchpin for organisational efficiency.

Vendor Managed Inventory, often referred to as VMI, constitutes a synergistic modus operandi wherein the supplier assumes the onus for orchestrating and maintaining optimal inventory levels at the client's facility. This approach presents a conduit through which organisations can fine-tune their operational machinations, attenuate overhead costs, and amplify customer satisfaction metrics. Nevertheless, for organisations to exploit VMI's full gamut of advantages, an organisational culture imbued with the ethos of continuous improvement is non-negotiable.

The Symbiosis of Continuous Improvement and Inventory Optimisation

One of the most salient advantages engendered by the integration of continuous improvement within VMI processes is the capability for perpetual optimisation of inventory metrics. Through meticulous scrutiny of demand oscillations, procurement lead times, and a suite of other Key Performance Indicators (KPIs), organisations are empowered to discern avenues for incremental enhancements. The actuation of such adjustments can precipitate improvements in inventory precision and product availability, culminating in a diminution of stockout occurrences, augmentation of fill rates, and, as a corollary, enhancement of customer satisfaction indices.

Analytical Identification and Eradication of Operational Inefficiencies

Furthermore, the advocacy for continuous improvement in VMI enables an incisive examination of operational mechanics, thereby furnishing organisations with the analytical tools required for the identification and subsequent elimination of procedural inefficiencies. By methodically parsing data and assorted performance metrics, both warehouse and inventory management professionals are poised to detect potential bottlenecks, redundant processes, and other forms of operational profligacy. This capacity for analytical oversight facilitates judicious decision-making aimed at procedural streamlining, cost mitigation, and the elevation of holistic operational efficacy.

Enhancing Supplier-Customer Collaboration Through Performance Metric Analysis

An additional salient facet of continuous improvement in VMI is its propensity to catalyse and fortify collaborative initiatives between the customer and the supplier. In undertaking periodic assessments of performance metrics, coupled with the reciprocation of best practices and the synchronisation of objectives and goals, organisations can cultivate mutually beneficial partnerships that are inherently predisposed towards continuous improvement. This symbiotic relationship proffers fertile grounds for the discovery of opportunities for process refinement, and paves the way for the co-creation of avant-garde solutions that yield mutual dividends.

Technological Infrastructure: The Backbone of Continuous Improvement in VMI

For the successful deployment and sustenance of continuous improvement methodologies within VMI frameworks, an investment in robust technological infrastructure is imperative. Utilising cutting-edge inventory management systems endowed with real-time data visualisation and analytics capabilities, organisations can distill actionable insights into demand dynamics and unveil hitherto unidentified optimisation opportunities. Moreover, these advanced systems serve as conduits for fostering seamless communication streams between the customer and supplier, thereby reinforcing the collaborative underpinnings of VMI and facilitating the unhindered interchange of critical information.

Conclusion: Realising the Pinnacle of Operational Excellence Through Continuous Improvement in VMI

In summation, the ethos of continuous improvement serves as a critical fulcrum in actualising the latent potential encapsulated within Vendor Managed Inventory processes. By ingraining a culture predicated on incessant refinement, organisations stand to benefit from optimised inventory levels, operational efficiency, and synergistic supplier-customer relationships. Coupled with judicious investments in state-of-the-art technology and analytical tools, stakeholders encompassing warehouse managers, inventory management professionals, and supply chain practitioners can holistically elevate the practice of continuous improvement, thereby unlocking unprecedented levels of efficiency within their respective organisations.

8. CHAPTER 8: INVENTORY OPTIMISATION IN E-COMMERCE AND OMNI-CHANNEL RETAILING

Unique Challenges in E-commerce Inventory Management

In the contemporary commercial ecosystem, which is underpinned by rapid technological advancements and shifts in consumer behavior, e-commerce has ascended as a paradigm-altering force. It has fundamentally transformed not just the mechanics of consumer interaction, but also how enterprises conceive and execute business strategies. With the advent of online shopping, commercial enterprises have been empowered to transcend geographical boundaries, exponentially widen their customer demographic, and amplify revenue streams. Despite the plethora of opportunities afforded by e-commerce, warehouse managers, inventory specialists, and supply chain practitioners are compelled to navigate an intricate web of challenges unique to digital inventory management.

The Imperative of Real-Time Inventory Visibility

A salient challenge in the e-commerce inventory management landscape is the imperative for real-time visibility of stock levels. In contrast to traditional brick-and-mortar establishments where inventory is physically present and can be manually counted, e-commerce platforms operate within the digital realm. This necessitates an acute requirement for precise, real-time data pertaining to product availability. To address this, it is incumbent upon inventory managers to implement robust inventory tracking systems characterised by high degrees of accuracy and reliability. These systems must be capable of seamless integration with online sales platforms and should be engineered to update inventory data instantaneously. A failure in achieving this pivotal component could manifest in a cascade of negative outcomes, including customer dissatisfaction, diminished sales, and irreparable damage to brand integrity.

Complexity of Order Fulfilment

A further layer of complexity is added by the intricacies involved in e-commerce order fulfilment. With orders often originating from disparate digital channels, inventory managers are faced with the Herculean task of ensuring that each order is not just processed but also shipped within an optimal timeframe. To tackle this, there needs to be a concerted effort to streamline warehouse operational flows, implement data-driven strategies to optimize the picking and packing procedures, and leverage advanced automation technologies such as robotics and conveyor systems. The exigencies of peak shopping seasons further exacerbate these complexities, making it imperative for businesses to employ strategic foresight in capacity planning to preempt stock-outs and maintain customer satisfaction levels.

Proliferation of SKUs and Product Variants

The e-commerce model allows businesses the luxury of offering a virtually limitless array of products, unconstrained by physical shelf space. While this may enhance customer choice, it adds an additional layer of complexity in inventory management. Inventory managers must engage in meticulous planning to organize and categorize an extensive catalog of SKUs (Stock Keeping Units) and their myriad variations. Furthermore, they must utilize sophisticated algorithms and analytics tools to accurately forecast demand patterns for each specific product, thereby enabling more intelligent, real-time decision-making in inventory level adjustments. Advanced inventory management software applications can automate these complex processes, thereby augmenting the efficiency of stock level management and mitigating the risks associated with overstocking or stock-outs.

The Challenge of Returns and Reverse Logistics

Finally, e-commerce business models are frequently accompanied by consumer expectations of lenient return policies and expedited refunds. This mandates that inventory managers evolve a robust framework for reverse logistics, facilitating efficient handling of returned merchandise. Processes must be put in place to accurately assess the condition of returned items, thereby determining whether they are fit for resale or require disposal. Proper management of this aspect not only amplifies customer satisfaction but also minimizes the adverse financial implications of product returns on the enterprise.

To summarise, the realm of e-commerce inventory management presents a complex tapestry of unique challenges that warehouse managers, inventory specialists, and supply chain practitioners must adeptly navigate. Core areas necessitating meticulous planning and strategic implementation include real-time inventory visibility, intricate order fulfilment processes, management of a diverse range of SKUs, and the efficient orchestration of reverse logistics. By proactively adopting advanced inventory management technologies, optimising warehouse operational efficiencies, and crafting intelligent reverse logistics policies, businesses can unlock unprecedented levels of efficiency in e-commerce inventory management. This will empower them to sustain a competitive edge in the increasingly volatile and competitive digital marketplace.

Multi-Channel Fulfillment Strategies: An Analytical Framework for the Integration and Optimisation of Diverse Sales Platforms

In the contemporary, rapid-paced commercial landscape, enterprises confront the intricate task of serving an ever-diversifying consumer populace. The modern consumer not only anticipates but essentially demands that orders be fulfilled through an assortment of channels—ranging from digital marketplaces and traditional brick-and-mortar establishments to emerging platforms like social media. Given this shifting terrain, it becomes imperative for warehouse and inventory managers to ingeniously devise and implement efficacious multi-channel fulfillment strategies.

A multi-channel fulfilment strategy is not merely a convergence of multiple sales channels; rather, it is a sophisticated orchestration aimed at ensuring an uninterrupted, seamless order fulfilment cycle. This symbiotic integration offers organisations the ability to penetrate broader market segments and exploit untapped revenue avenues. However, the successful operationalisation of such a strategy mandates meticulous planning and the strategic employment of advanced inventory management methodologies.

A cornerstone of this multi-faceted approach is the concept of "Inventory Visibility." For effective governance of inventory across diversified channels, it is critical for warehouse managers to possess a real-time, panoramic view of stock levels. To this end, leveraging specialised inventory management software that affords a unified, holistic view and seamlessly integrates with each discrete sales channel is instrumental. Such systems empower managers to make data-driven decisions, thereby mitigating the risks of both stock-outs and overstocks.

Streamlining the operational elements of multi-channel fulfilment is yet another imperative. Best practices in this domain include the integration of automated order processing systems, often employing advanced technologies like robotics for order picking and packaging. Such automation not only enhances accuracy but significantly augments order-processing speed. Moreover, centralising order management systems can act as a fulcrum to amalgamate orders from disparate channels, thereby mitigating operational complexity and assuring timely order execution.

Furthermore, logistics management stands as a paramount component in the multi-channel fulfilment equation. This entails optimising not only the physical routes through which products are transported but also the selection of the most cost-effective and reliable carriers. Forming strategic alliances with third-party logistics providers, who bring specialised expertise in managing complex multi-channel fulfilment matrices, can offer invaluable synergies.

Attention to customer experience transcends mere nicety to become a categorical imperative in building and sustaining customer loyalty. Achieving a seamless, cross-channel experience is indispensable. This is exemplified by innovative options such as click-and-collect services, enabling consumers to blend digital ease with physical accessibility. Timely and accurate order-tracking mechanisms further enhance consumer engagement by maintaining transparency throughout the fulfilment lifecycle.

In summation, mastering multi-channel fulfilment strategies is no longer a choice but a requisite for organisations aiming to navigate the complex choreography of modern consumer demands. Through prioritisation of inventory visibility, operational streamlining, logistics optimisation, and a customer-centric approach, businesses can elevate supply chain efficiencies and carve out a robust competitive position in an ever-fluid marketplace.

Inventory Allocation and Network Optimisation: A Synthesis of Best Practices for Supply Chain Efficiency

In an era marked by intense market competition, the role of strategic inventory management in establishing and maintaining a competitive advantage has never been more pivotal. Practitioners in Warehouse Management, Inventory Management, and Supply Chain Management are confronted with multifaceted challenges requiring perpetual optimisation. This subchapter elucidates the sophisticated methodologies underlying inventory allocation and network optimisation, with the intention of providing actionable insights for professionals aiming to optimize their supply chain processes.

Inventory allocation is an orchestrated methodology, underpinned by analytics, aimed at optimal distribution of inventory across a diverse set of locations within an intricate supply chain network. It calls for the adoption of data-driven decision-making paradigms that factor in a multitude of variables—cost structures, service level objectives, and lead times—aiming to ensure that inventory is judiciously situated in time, place, and quantity. By minimising the likelihood of stock-outs and excess inventory, effective inventory allocation acts as a linchpin for operational efficiency.

Conversely, network optimisation focuses on the architectural design and configuration of the supply chain network itself. Through a rigorous analysis of multiple variables—including transportation expenditures, customer demand fluctuations, and the capacity of various facilities—network optimisation endeavours to architect an efficacious supply chain network. This encompasses the strategic location and number of warehouses, distribution centers, and retail outlets, as well as the determination of the most efficient transportation modalities and routes.

Cutting-edge analytics and forecasting techniques, such as machine learning algorithms, can offer unparalleled insights into demand patterns, enabling precise inventory level optimisation. Moreover, fostering a collaborative environment with robust information sharing across the supply chain network can significantly amplify both visibility and responsiveness.

The role of technological innovation in inventory management and network optimisation cannot be overstated. Advanced systems—encompassing Inventory Management Systems (IMS), Warehouse Management Systems (WMS), and Transportation Management Systems (TMS)—automate intricate processes, thereby elevating accuracy and facilitating intelligent decision-making.

Incorporating empirical case studies and best practice exemplars throughout this subchapter will serve to bridge the gap between theoretical frameworks and practical implementation. Through this, professionals in Warehouse

Management, Inventory Management, and Supply Chain Management can acquire invaluable tools and insights that can be directly applied to enhance operational efficiencies, reduce overall costs, and elevate customer satisfaction metrics.

In conclusion, this subchapter seeks to equip professionals with an enriched toolkit of methodologies and strategies that can unlock unprecedented efficiencies and secure a competitive advantage in an increasingly complex and challenging marketplace. By judiciously implementing state-of-the-art practices in inventory allocation and network optimisation, supply chain operations can be not merely optimised but, in fact, transformed.

Inventory Management in the Age of Digital Marketplaces: A Multifaceted Exploration

In the contemporary commercial environment, the ascendance of online marketplaces has engendered a paradigm shift in the manner in which businesses conduct their operations. The proliferation of e-commerce behemoths like Amazon and Alibaba has compelled traditional brick-and-mortar retailers to confront an increasingly arduous competitive landscape in the digital domain. Consequently, practitioners engaged in warehouse management, inventory control, and overarching supply chain management are obliged to recalibrate their operational strategies to adeptly navigate this novel landscape. The reverberations of this digital transformation on inventory management are both profound and far-reaching. This subchapter endeavours to furnish a nuanced understanding, proffer valuable insights, and delineate pragmatic strategies for optimising inventory management systems in the dynamic milieu of online marketplaces.

Demand Forecasting in the Digital Sphere

A salient facet of inventory management germane to this discussion is the art and science of demand forecasting. In an online marketplace, the vicissitudes of customer behavior render it extraordinarily unpredictable. Advanced analytical methodologies, such as data analytics and machine learning algorithms, assume a heightened level of significance in this context. By assiduously leveraging these sophisticated techniques, inventory managers can procure invaluable insights into consumer predilections and purchasing trajectories. Such empirical data facilitates nuanced inventory optimisation, ameliorating the perennial challenges of stock-outs and overstocking, thereby mitigating financial risk and enhancing operational efficiency.

Order Fulfilment and Customer Expectations

Inextricably linked with the above is the aspect of order fulfilment—a process undergoing monumental shifts owing to customer expectations set by online marketplaces. Consumers interacting with these platforms have grown accustomed to, and thus demand, rapid and dependable delivery services. For warehouse managers, this necessitates a radical overhaul of their extant order fulfilment paradigms. The incorporation of advanced Warehouse Management Systems (WMS), optimisation of picking and packing procedures, and strategic collaborations with logistics partners are pivotal to achieving the alacrity required to maintain a competitive stance in the digital arena. Speed and efficiency thus emerge not merely as operational objectives but as quintessential elements of a brand's value proposition in the online marketplace.

Navigating the Complexities of Product Returns

Inventory management is further complicated by the preponderance of product returns, a phenomenon accentuated by the often generous return policies of online marketplaces. In consequence, inventory managers are obliged to formulate robust processes for the expeditious handling of returns, efficient refurbishing of products, and the meticulous maintenance of inventory records to accurately reflect such reverse logistics activities. Through adept management of this intricate process, organisations can not only curtail the costs associated with returns but also sustain, if not augment, levels of customer satisfaction and brand loyalty.

The Imperative of Technological Leveraging

In this digitally interconnected age, the adoption of cutting-edge technology and automation techniques is no longer optional but a categorical imperative for inventory managers. Employing sophisticated inventory management software, incorporating tools such as barcode scanning and Radio-Frequency Identification (RFID) tagging, businesses can attain real-time visibility into their inventory states. The consequent data-rich environment empowers them to make informed, data-driven decisions that are instrumental in optimising inventory levels and thereby ameliorating overall supply chain efficiency.

Inventory management in the burgeoning arena of online marketplaces proffers both formidable challenges and lucrative opportunities for stakeholders in warehouse management, inventory control, and supply chain optimisation. By espousing avant-garde technologies, capitalising on data analytics, and rendering order fulfilment processes more streamlined and responsive, enterprises can engender operational efficiencies that serve as a springboard for gaining a sustainable competitive advantage in the perpetually evolving landscape of e-commerce.

9. CHAPTER 9: PERFORMANCE METRICS AND KPIS FOR INVENTORY MANAGEMENT

Performance Metrics and Key Performance Indicators (KPIs) in Inventory Management

The contemporary landscape of supply chain management is a complex ecosystem that demands an intricate balance of efficiency, cost-optimization, and customer satisfaction. At the fulcrum of this intricate balance is inventory management—a quintessential component of modern business operations that orchestrates the availability, cost, and location of products. Given the critical role that inventory plays, there is a compelling necessity for robust metrics and Key Performance Indicators (KPIs) to quantitatively assess the effectiveness and efficiency of inventory-related operations. This subchapter aims to explore and delineate the salient KPIs that warehouse managers, inventory managers, and practitioners of supply chain management should concentrate upon to optimize operational efficiency in inventory management.

Enumerating Key Performance Indicators for Inventory Management

- **Inventory Turnover Ratio:** This metric serves as an incisive indicator of the efficiency associated with the utilisation of inventory resources. It measures the frequency with which inventory assets are sold and replenished over a specified period. A high turnover ratio is often indicative of strong consumer demand, whereas a low turnover could imply stagnation, thereby locking up working capital and occupying warehouse space unnecessarily.

- **Stockout Rate:** This KPI quantifies the incidence of stock-outs—situations where the inventory is insufficient to meet customer demand. A high stockout rate is symptomatic of missed revenue generation opportunities and could lead to significant customer dissatisfaction, impacting long-term customer retention.
- **Perfect Order Fulfilment:** This KPI tracks the proportion of orders that are flawlessly executed in terms of accuracy, timeliness, and completeness. This metric is particularly instrumental in gauging the overall efficacy of inventory management protocols, thereby influencing customer satisfaction and engendering customer loyalty.
- **Carrying Cost of Inventory:** This is a composite metric that incorporates various expenditures associated with holding inventory, such as costs pertaining to storage, insurance, obsolescence, and depreciation. Monitoring this KPI can reveal financial inefficiencies and offer strategic insights into right-sizing inventory levels to minimize these costs.
- **Fill Rate:** Often expressed as a percentage, this KPI evaluates the extent to which customer orders can be immediately satisfied from existing inventory. A high fill rate usually signifies an effective inventory management system, whereas a low fill rate could indicate potential bottlenecks in the supply chain.
- **Order Cycle Time:** This KPI monitors the temporal interval that elapses from the initiation of an order to its ultimate fulfilment. Minimising order cycle time is critical for achieving customer satisfaction in an age where expedited delivery is often a competitive differentiator.
- **Backorder Rate:** Measuring the proportion of orders that cannot be fulfilled instantly due to inventory limitations, this KPI underscores the need for robust demand forecasting techniques, optimised replenishment strategies, and agile production planning.

By meticulously tracking these KPIs, stakeholders across various echelons of supply chain management can garner nuanced insights into the state of inventory management within their organisations. These metrics collectively contribute to a panoramic view of inventory performance, thereby empowering decision-makers with the analytical acumen necessary for continuous operational refinement.

A Deeper Dive into Measuring Inventory Turnover

Inventory turnover stands as a pivotal metric in the inventory management domain, serving as a critical measure of how successfully an enterprise manages the dichotomy of meeting consumer demand and optimizing inventory levels. For individuals in key roles such as warehouse managers, inventory managers, and supply chain specialists, mastering the art and science of inventory turnover measurement is indispensable for operational excellence.

Several methodologies can be employed to calculate inventory turnover; however, the most widely utilised formula involves dividing the Cost of Goods Sold (COGS) by the Average Inventory for a given period. Here, COGS encapsulates the direct costs implicated in the production or acquisition of the goods that are sold, while Average Inventory reflects the mean value of the inventory over the specified timeframe.

A nuanced analysis of inventory turnover can furnish insights into various operational aspects. For instance, a high turnover ratio suggests a streamlined supply chain, strong market demand, and efficient inventory practices. Conversely, a low turnover ratio could be a red flag, signalling inefficiencies that lock valuable financial resources in slow-moving or obsolete inventory.

Furthermore, understanding inventory turnover transcends merely assessing the velocity of stock movement; it also enables proactive identification of potential systemic issues, such as recurrent stock-outs or inventory surpluses. By leveraging this KPI, decision-makers can fine-tune inventory par levels to align with demand patterns, thus mitigating risks associated with overstocking or under-stocking.

Beyond its role as a standalone metric, inventory turnover serves as an integrative gauge for evaluating overarching supply chain performance. Longitudinal tracking of this KPI can illuminate the efficacy of process enhancements, the accuracy of demand forecasts, and the quality of supplier interactions, thereby furnishing a multidimensional view of supply chain health.

Inventory turnover, along with the other Key Performance Indicators elucidated herein, offers a quantifiable framework for evaluating and enhancing inventory management practices. Mastery of these metrics allows warehouse managers, inventory managers, and supply chain practitioners to embark on data-driven journeys toward operational optimisation. By assiduously monitoring these metrics, organisations can not only enrich customer satisfaction but also engender cost efficiencies, thereby securing a competitive advantage in an increasingly volatile and complex market environment.

Fill Rate and Perfect Order Performance: Integral Components for Supply Chain Efficacy

In the intricate landscape of supply chain management, the twin metrics of fill rate and perfect order performance stand out as critical markers for gauging operational efficiency and organizational success. These metrics serve as compasses for professionals—ranging from warehouse managers to inventory supervisors and experts in supply chain management—in navigating the complexities of inventory management. This subchapter aims to dissect the foundational principles behind fill rate and perfect order performance, scrutinize their role in inventory management, and articulate strategies for optimizing these essential Key Performance Indicators (KPIs).

Conceptual Framework of Fill Rate

Fill rate is conceptually framed as the ratio—expressed as a percentage—of customer demand that is successfully met through immediately available stock. This metric not only quantifies an organisation's competence in satisfying customer demands in a timely manner but also serves as an indicator of the efficacy of inventory control systems. Elevated fill rates are often synonymous with heightened levels of customer satisfaction and sustained customer loyalty. As such, warehouse managers should tirelessly strive to elevate fill rates by implementing a multi-pronged approach that entails meticulous monitoring of inventory levels, accurate demand forecasting, and adept management of replenishment mechanisms.

The Imperative of Perfect Order Performance

Perfect order performance is quantified as the ratio of orders that are impeccably executed, devoid of any errors including but not limited to incorrect item allocation, tardy deliveries, or merchandise impairments. The attainment of elevated levels of perfect order performance is a non-negotiable requisite for solidifying a robust organisational reputation and engendering enduring customer trust. Warehouse and inventory managers should focus on the multi-dimensional aspects of order accuracy, procedural efficiency in order processing, and the institution of comprehensive quality control protocols.

Strategies for Optimisation

Optimising fill rate and perfect order performance requires an intricate blend of strategies:

- **Demand Forecasting:** Accurate demand prediction is pivotal for ensuring the availability of pertinent merchandise at opportune times. Managers should employ data analytics tools and algorithms to scrutinise historical sales data, liaise with sales divisions, and utilize advanced predictive modeling to anticipate consumer behavior.

- **Inventory Optimisation Techniques:** Initiatives such as safety stock management and cross-docking contribute to improving fill rates. Calculating optimal safety stock levels contingent on historical demand fluctuations and supply lead times can mitigate the risk of stock-outs. Concurrently, the deployment of cross-docking operations expedites order fulfilment by circumventing conventional put-away and picking procedures.

- **Operational Efficiency:** Automated order processing systems and cutting-edge technological solutions can exponentially augment perfect order performance. Managers should focus on minimising latency in order processing through automation and enforce rigorous quality assurance checks at various junctures in the supply chain.

- **Performance Monitoring:** The perpetual surveillance of performance metrics associated with fill rate and perfect order performance serves as an invaluable tool for isolating areas that demand improvement. Metrics such as order accuracy rate, on-time delivery quotient, and backorder prevalence should be continuously scrutinised to identify operational inefficiencies and formulate corrective measures.

In summation, fill rate and perfect order performance are cardinal KPIs that shape the landscape of inventory management. Professionals across various echelons of supply chain management should focus their energies on finessing these metrics through the adroit implementation of demand forecasting methodologies, inventory optimisation paradigms, and advanced operational processes. This integrated approach can unlock unparalleled efficiencies in supply chain operations and engender streamlined inventory management frameworks.

Continuous Improvement through Performance Metrics: A Methodological Approach

The implementation of performance metrics serves as the cornerstone for perpetuating iterative improvements in inventory management and engenders holistic optimization of the entire supply chain ecosystem. Stakeholders including warehouse managers, inventory supervisors, and supply chain management experts, are cognizant of the imperative nature of employing these performance metrics as diagnostic tools for operational betterment. This subchapter delineates the invaluable role performance metrics play, elucidates the methodologies to leverage them for continuous improvement, and enumerates specific metrics germane to distinct inventory management paradigms.

The Utility of Performance Metrics

Performance metrics function as quantifiable proxies that allow for the systematic appraisal of the efficacy of inventory management systems. These metrics empower warehouse supervisors and other stakeholders to unveil bottlenecks, pinpoint inefficiencies, and isolate areas ripe for improvement. Performance indicators span a continuum from rudimentary metrics such as order accuracy and on-time delivery rates, to more intricate parameters like the inventory turnover ratio and the carrying cost of stock.

Analytical Approaches for Continuous Improvement

The interpretive analysis of performance metrics enables managerial staff to locate and concentrate on areas that warrant strategic improvements. For instance, if the evaluation of metrics reveals a burdensome carrying cost of inventory, action plans can be devised to pare down surplus stock or refine demand forecasting algorithms to minimize holding expenses. Conversely, if metrics indicate subpar order accuracy, robust quality control protocols can be inaugurated to ameliorate accuracy and curtail customer dissatisfaction, or the cost associated with returns.

Niche-Specific Performance Metrics

The selection of performance metrics must be custom-tailored to the unique characteristics of distinct inventory management sub-domains. In a Just-In-Time (JIT) inventory framework, the salient metrics may encompass stockout rate, order cycle durations, and lead time variability, which collectively work towards ensuring seamless material flow and inventory accessibility. Conversely, in high-throughput, low-margin inventory environments, relevant metrics could include the inventory turnover ratio, fill rates, and the accuracy of order picking among others.

Performance metrics serve as indispensable levers for instigating a culture of continuous improvement within the realm of inventory management. By astutely employing these metrics, warehouse managers, inventory supervisors, and supply chain professionals can not only identify areas for iterative betterment but can also instantiate cost-effective, streamlined, and customer-centric operations. The imperative, however, is to judiciously select metrics that align with the idiosyncrasies of specific inventory management models to yield actionable insights that drive genuine operational improvements.

In conclusion, the concept of continuous improvement via the deployment of performance metrics constitutes an indispensable element of contemporary inventory management practices. Through careful metric selection and data-driven analytics, organisations can elucidate opportunities for process enhancements, cost mitigation, and ultimately, achieve superior levels of efficiency across their supply chain operations.

10. CHAPTER 10: IMPLEMENTING SUPPLY CHAIN OPTIMISATION STRATEGIES

Assessing Current Inventory Management Practices

In an increasingly complex and volatile commercial landscape, the indispensability of proficient inventory management for the prosperity of contemporary organizations is more accentuated than ever. The triumvirate of Warehouse Managers, Inventory Managers, and Supply Chain Management Practitioners act as the linchpins in the pursuit of optimized inventory management and the augmentation of supply chain efficacy. This subchapter endeavors to proffer comprehensive, actionable intelligence for these professionals to critically assess the extant paradigms of inventory management, thereby illuminating avenues for process enhancement and the full actualization of supply chain capabilities.

To inaugurate, a meticulous evaluation of the prevalent inventory management practices serves as an invaluable mechanism for the identification of systemic inefficiencies, lacunae, or sub-optimal processes. This evaluative process can be implemented through a multi-pronged approach: conducting rigorous physical audits, the scrutiny of quantifiable data and analytic reports, and fostering dialogues with germane stakeholders across the organisational ecosystem. Through the synthesis of these multifarious evaluative methodologies, practitioners are endowed with an encyclopaedic grasp of the current inventory management topology, thereby capacitating them to pinpoint bottlenecks, superfluous inventory, or material deficits and strategise interventions.

A salient component of this diagnostic process is the deployment of benchmarking protocols. The juxtaposition of an organisation's inventory management metrics against industry pacesetters and established best practices imbues vital context to the assessment. This involves the critical examination of Key Performance Indicators (KPIs)—such as inventory turnover ratios, stock accuracy percentages, order fulfilment rates, and the financial metrics of carrying costs. By conducting comparative analyses against these normative benchmarks, practitioners can diagnose performance discrepancies and formulate remedial strategies to ameliorate these gaps.

Contemporaneously, a critical inspection of the extant technological infrastructure is instrumental. This entails an audit of the efficaciousness and precision of the inventory tracking systems, the sophistication of order management software, and the predictive accuracy of forecasting algorithms and tools. The discernment of technological shortcomings empowers professionals to investigate cutting-edge, technologically superior alternatives that may yield substantial improvements in operational efficiency and cost-effectiveness.

Moreover, an often-underemphasised aspect of inventory management assessment is the exogenous variables, including fluctuating customer expectations, evolving market dynamics, and stringent regulatory impositions. Acquiring insights into these external variables aids practitioners in recalibrating their inventory management paradigms to ensure alignment and responsiveness. For example, a shift in consumer preference toward expedited delivery could necessitate the adaptation of nimble inventory strategies like Just-in-Time (JIT) or Vendor-Managed Inventory (VMI).

In summation, the critical assessment of prevailing inventory management practices is a sine qua non for Warehouse Managers, Inventory Managers, and Supply Chain Management Practitioners. By amalgamating a comprehensive evaluation process, industry benchmarking, technological scrutiny, and the consideration of external variables, these professionals can identify focal points for enhancement and unlock operational efficiencies within their inventory management ecosystems. This subchapter aspires to arm these practitioners with an arsenal of intellectual resources and methodological tools for the attainment of inventory management excellence.

Developing an Inventory Optimisation Strategy

In the fiercely competitive business milieu of today, the overarching need for incisive inventory management strategies is not just a luxury but an operational imperative for organizations aiming for peak efficiency and cost minimization. Warehouse Managers, Inventory Managers, and Supply Chain Management Practitioners thus find themselves tasked with the formulation of robust, sustainable inventory optimization strategies. This subchapter aims to demystify the composite elements and sequential steps requisite for the formulation of such strategies, thereby capacitating professionals in the domain of inventory management with the erudition and practical know-how requisite for organizational success.

As an antecedent to the strategy development process, it is imperative to coherently comprehend and articulate the organisational objectives and fiscal imperatives. This alignment ensures that the ensuing inventory management paradigms and initiatives are intrinsically contributory to the fulfilment of the organisational strategic blueprint. This involves a granular examination of customer demand oscillations, sales trajectory projections, and market fluxes to deduce the quintessential inventory composition and product assortments.

After the establishment of these guiding objectives, a comprehensive inventory analysis represents the next critical juncture. This analysis entails the segmentation of inventory pools predicated on attributes such as monetary value, demand variability, and procurement lead times. This taxonomic exercise enables managers to allocate resources and management bandwidth with surgical precision, based on inventory attributes. For instance, items classified as high-value and exhibiting rapid inventory turns may necessitate elevated safety stock thresholds to forestall stock-outs, whereas slow-moving items may be candidates for de-listing or targeted promotional activities.

Following this inventory analysis, practitioners can then commence the actualisation of various optimisation mechanisms. These may encompass advanced demand forecasting models predicated on machine learning algorithms, empirical safety stock computations, and Economic Order Quantity (EOQ) methodologies that consider both holding and ordering costs. The integration of sophisticated inventory management software platforms can exponentially augment the efficiency of these tasks by furnishing real-time data analytics, and algorithmic inventory level optimisation capabilities.

To validate and perpetuate the efficacy of the inventory optimisation strategy, continuous performance measurement is non-negotiable. This is operationalised through the persistent tracking of Key Performance Indicators (KPIs) such as inventory turnover velocities, order fill rates, and stock veracity indices. Continuous surveillance of these metrics furnishes managers with actionable insights for iterative strategy refinement.

In addition, achieving the pinnacle of inventory optimisation is rarely a solitary endeavour; rather, it mandates collaborative synergies with pivotal organisational stakeholders, encompassing suppliers and sales teams. By engendering data transparency and strategic alignment with these entities, practitioners can actualize significant advancements in forecast fidelity, lead time compression, and overall supply chain fluidity.

In conclusion, the concoction of an efficacious inventory optimisation strategy is an operational exigency for Warehouse Managers, Inventory Managers, and Supply Chain Management Practitioners. Through an integrated approach that incorporates the alignment with organizational objectives, a thorough inventory analysis, the adoption of state-of-the-art optimisation techniques, relentless performance tracking, and cross-functional collaboration, professionals can unlock latent efficiencies and orchestrate sustained success in their inventory management practices.

Change Management and Implementation Challenges within Inventory Management

In the ever-evolving landscape of supply chain management, businesses invariably confront an inherent flux, necessitating periodic alterations in strategies and technological adoptions. This subchapter delves deeper into the nuanced facets of change management and its ramifications, exploring the attendant challenges experienced by the vanguards of inventory control, namely warehouse managers, inventory specialists, and supply chain management connoisseurs.

Change management can be succinctly defined as the methodical modus operandi of transitioning entities, be they individuals, teams, or entire organisations, from a prevailing status quo to an envisaged future state. This intricate process mandates meticulous planning, consistent and effective communication, and adept execution, all aimed at achieving seamless transition whilst ensuring the regular operations remain unfettered. For those steering the helm of inventory control, mastering the tenets of change management becomes imperative to facilitate the efficacious introduction of avant-garde inventory management paradigms.

A perennial challenge in the realm of change management is the proclivity towards inertia and resistance to change. Entrenched in their familiarity with extant processes and technological tools, employees may exhibit reluctance to onboard novel methodologies. This inertia can be mitigated through strategic communication, comprehensive training, and by endorsing a participatory approach, granting employees a voice in the decision-making continuum.

Yet another formidable challenge lies in the amalgamation of emergent technologies with legacy systems. As inventory management systems undergo metamorphosis or as automation takes precedence, the task becomes labyrinthine and demands significant temporal investments. The stewards of inventory control, namely warehouse and inventory managers, are entrusted with the onus of ensuring seamless technological integration. Such endeavours often warrant synergies with IT contingents and technological vendors to triumph over potential integration impediments.

Beyond the technological ambit, change management is also ensnared in the quagmire of aligning the organisation's ethos with the proposed alterations. Such alignment predicates on visionary leadership and dynamic change agents capable of galvanising the workforce towards assimilating and championing the change. Cultivating an organizational milieu that celebrates ceaseless refinement and innovation becomes instrumental in the triumphant realisation of cutting-edge inventory management techniques.

A prudent change management strategy also warrants scrutiny of the fiscal ramifications accompanying proposed shifts. Allotting funds for technological advancements, capacity building initiatives, and the interim operational inefficiencies during the transitory phase become paramount. Thus, those at the forefront of inventory control need to judiciously evaluate the return on investment, ensuring the resultant benefits supersede the incurred expenditure.

To surmount these multifaceted challenges, it becomes paramount to architect a holistic change management blueprint. Encompassing explicit goals, a structured timeline, communication blueprints, capacity building initiatives, and performance metrics, this plan becomes the lodestar guiding the change process. Periodic oversight and feedback mechanisms help in early detection and rectification of discrepancies, ensuring the fruition of the envisaged objectives.

In summation, the labyrinth of change management and concomitant implementation hurdles is an intrinsic facet of inventory management. Those steering the ship must be well-versed in change management doctrines, adept at addressing employee inertia, technological assimilation challenges, cultural realignments, and fiscal implications. A proactive approach ensures operational efficiency in inventory management, propelling businesses to the zenith in an intensely competitive marketplace.

Monitoring and Continuous Improvement: The Bedrock of Optimisation

The frenetic and hyper-competitive milieu of supply chain management underscores the imperative of relentless monitoring and iterative refinement of optimization endeavours. The custodians of inventory control, encompassing Warehouse Managers, Inventory Managers, and Supply Chain Management mavens, must internalize the ethos that optimization is an iterative continuum, demanding unwavering oversight and perpetual enhancement.

Optimisation is a tripartite process, beginning with the identification of performance bottlenecks, followed by strategy formulation and its subsequent implementation, and culminating in an assessment of the outcomes. However, this is not a terminus; the cyclical nature of optimisation mandates sustained vigilance over the instituted measures, ensuring they yield the envisaged dividends and flagging emergent enhancement avenues.

A cardinal element in this optimisation odyssey is data-driven decision-making. Those helming inventory control must leverage sophisticated analytical apparatuses to collate intricate data, spanning metrics such as order fulfilment ratios, stock veracity, operational cycle durations, and supply lead times, to name a few.

By subjecting this voluminous data to rigorous analytical scrutiny, discerning managers can unearth emergent patterns, discern trends, and pinpoint potential chokepoints impeding operational fluidity. Such insights empower managers to institute targeted rectifications. For instance, recurrent stockout instances for specific inventory items could necessitate recalibration of reorder thresholds or the exploration of alternate vendor alliances.

In parallel, an optimisation framework also necessitates forging feedback channels with a myriad of stakeholders – from internal employees to external partners like customers and suppliers. These feedback loops often unveil a plethora of insights, illuminating potential enhancements that might elude even the most rigorous data analytics.

At the heart of this optimisation pilgrimage is the spirit of continuous improvement. Those in leadership roles within inventory control must endeavour to inculcate an organisational culture that reveres and champions this ethos. Such a culture germinates from a consistent evaluation of instituted strategies, fostering employee-driven innovation, and investing in capacity-building initiatives to augment organisational competencies.

To encapsulate, relentless monitoring paired with a commitment to continuous refinement stands as the linchpin of achieving and sustaining inventory management excellence. Through data-driven strategies, active stakeholder engagement, and an unwavering commitment to improvement, the custodians of inventory can unleash the latent potential of their supply chains, ensuring a vanguard position in a globally competitive marketplace.

11. CHAPTER 11: EMPIRICAL ANALYSES OF SUPPLY CHAIN OPTIMISATION STRATEGIES

Case Study 1: Augmenting Operational Efficiency through Sophisticated Demand Forecasting Mechanisms

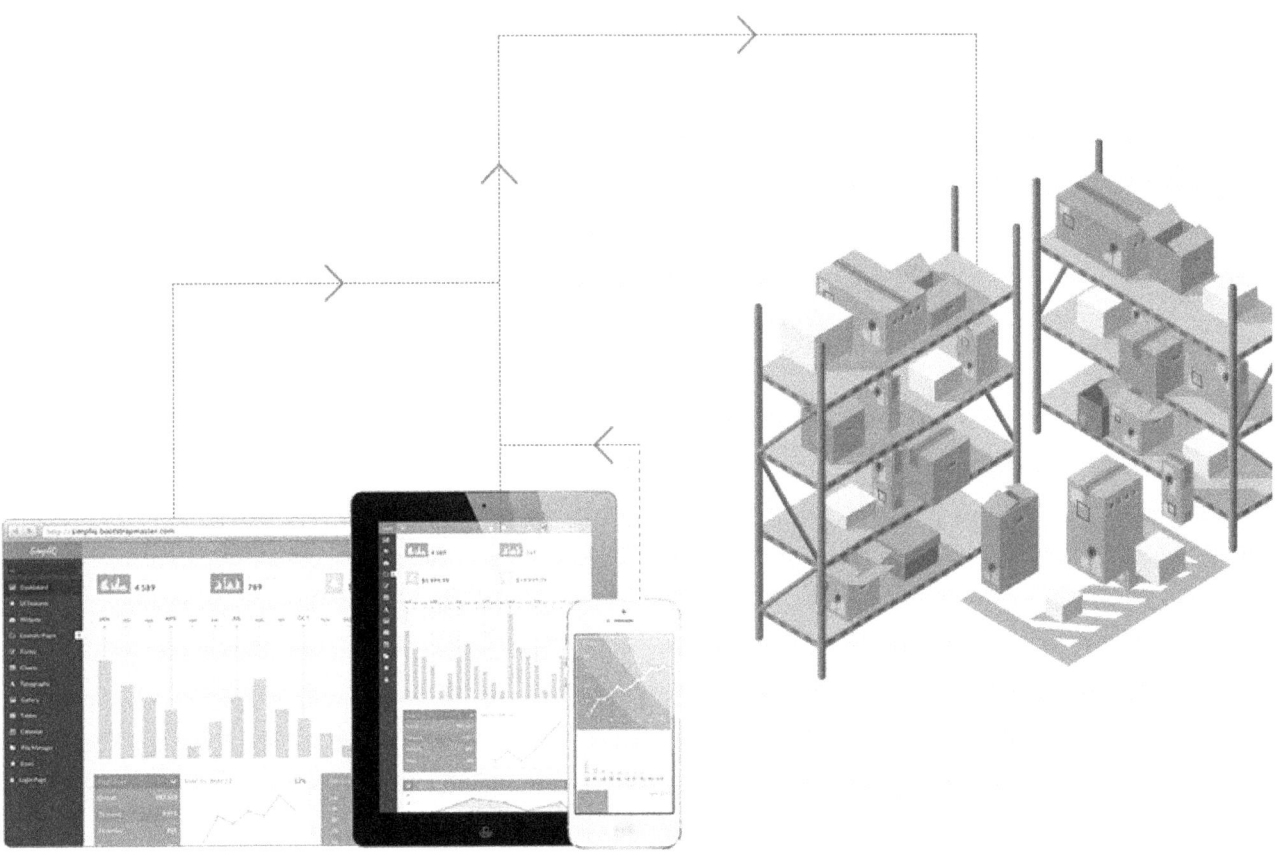

In this in-depth chapter, we endeavour to dissect an illustrative real-world case study that elucidates the profound implications of demand forecasting on the enhancement of supply chain operational efficiency. This empirical analysis explores, in granular detail, the strategic endeavours of a particular organisation that achieved a marked improvement in its inventory management processes by judiciously employing a panoply of demand forecasting techniques. The chapter aims to furnish Warehouse Managers, Inventory Managers, and Supply Chain Management Practitioners with invaluable insights into the transformative potential of demand forecasting for streamlining inventory management frameworks.

Background and Problem Identification

The organisation under examination was beleaguered with an array of formidable challenges directly pertaining to inventory management. On the one end of the spectrum, excessive stockpiling engendered elevated carrying costs, thus exacerbating capital allocation inefficiencies. Concurrently, the organisation faced spatial constraints within its warehousing facilities. On the opposite end, stock-outs were recurrent phenomena, engendering customer dissatisfaction and consequently resulting in missed revenue-generating opportunities. Recognising these quandaries as symptoms of sub-optimal inventory management strategies, the firm decided to embark upon a focused initiative to harness demand forecasting as an analytic instrument for refining its inventory management schema.

Methodological Implementation

To undertake this ambitious endeavor, the company initiated the process by scrupulously amassing a longitudinal dataset that comprised historical sales metrics and fluctuating patterns of customer demand. This raw data was subsequently subjected to rigorous analysis by deploying a suite of advanced statistical methodologies and data-driven forecasting algorithms. The final demand forecasting model was meticulously calibrated to incorporate a diverse array of salient variables including, but not limited to, seasonality, longitudinal trends, promotional campaigns, and prevailing external market exigencies. By cultivating an astute understanding of projected demand patterns, the organization was capacitated to make data-driven judgments relating to procurement strategies, production planning, and the calibration of optimal inventory levels.

Results and Operational Impact

The concretisation of demand forecasting mechanisms engendered a transformative impact on the organisation's operational efficiency and financial performance. With the newfound capability to generate robust demand forecasts, the company optimised its inventory holdings, thereby attenuating carrying costs and liberating valuable warehouse space. Moreover, by virtue of these predictive insights, the firm was also able to revamp its procurement protocols, thereby diminishing lead times and substantially mitigating the incidence of stock-outs. These operational refinements culminated in elevated levels of customer satisfaction and materialised in enhanced revenue generation capabilities.

Key Takeaways: Lessons for the Industry

The present case study serves to underline the cardinal significance of demand forecasting in the modern landscape of inventory management. Warehouse Managers, Inventory Managers, and Supply Chain Management Practitioners stand to glean several critical lessons from this empirical exploration:

- Precision in demand forecasting engenders a potent lever for the optimisation of inventory levels, thereby curtailing carrying costs and releasing warehousing space for more strategic uses.

- A proactive stance in demand forecasting empowers organisations to enact anticipatory procurement and production planning, thus averting stockouts and incrementally enhancing customer satisfaction indices.

- The deployment of advanced statistical and computational models, supplemented by cutting-edge forecasting algorithms, remains indispensable for generating accurate projections of future demand, especially when considering multi-dimensional factors such as seasonality, cyclical market trends, and promotional activities.

- The institutionalisation of demand forecasting paradigms mandates the systematic collection and analytical scrutiny of historical sales and demand data for the calibration of predictive models endowed with high degrees of reliability and robustness.

In summation, demand forecasting emerges as an invaluable tactical asset for catalysing supply chain optimisation, with particular emphasis on the domain of inventory management. The presented case study serves as a tangible testament to the monumental efficiency gains and profitability enhancements that organisations can achieve through the astute application of demand forecasting mechanisms. Warehouse Managers, Inventory Managers, and Supply Chain Management Practitioners are strongly encouraged to extrapolate these strategic insights to facilitate a reengineering of their inventory management paradigms, thereby unlocking new vistas of operational efficiency and overarching business success.

Case Study 2: Implementing Just-In-Time (JIT) Inventory Management: A Critical Analysis of Operational Efficiency and Strategic Approaches

In the labyrinthine world of supply chain management, the role of inventory management is often of paramount significance, constituting a linchpin that can either elevate or impede the efficiency of the overall supply chain framework. Specifically tailored to address the informational needs of warehouse managers, inventory coordinators, and supply chain management professionals, the ensuing case study endeavours to elucidate the intricacies of successfully implementing Just-In-Time (JIT) inventory management systems. This research is structured to offer a compendium of valuable insights, pragmatic methodologies, and best practices aimed at fortifying inventory management protocols within a range of organisational settings.

The Imperatives of Inventory Management in Supply Chain Optimisation

Inventory management is not merely an operational adjunct but rather a critical facet that is inextricably tied to the vitality of supply chain functionality. It demands the meticulous execution of a balance—a balance that sways between the necessity to maintain optimum stock levels and the imperative to minimize superfluous inventory, which otherwise would ensnare capital and inflate operational expenditures. It is within this complex operational nexus that JIT inventory management manifests as a transformative paradigm, promulgating streamlined operational workflows and engendering heightened levels of efficiency.

Foundational Principles and Attributes of JIT Inventory Management

The cornerstone of this study shall be an expository elucidation of the foundational principles that undergird the JIT inventory management system. The exposition will delve into core concepts such as pull-based inventory, demand-driven resupply, and zero-buffer inventory strategies, all of which contribute to the overarching objectives of JIT. By dissecting these elements, warehouse management professionals will be equipped with a nuanced understanding of how JIT paradigms can metamorphose their operational frameworks to achieve heightened profitability through reduced carrying costs, minimised incidents of stock-outs, enhanced cash flow liquidity, and bolstered customer satisfaction indices.

A Pragmatic Analysis: Case Exemplar of a Successful JIT Implementation

The subsequent section of this study will feature an in-depth analytical evaluation of a real-world organisational model that has successfully harnessed the potential of JIT inventory management systems. The analysis will enumerate the multifaceted challenges encountered by the organisation, elucidate the strategic countermeasures deployed to surmount these impediments, and delineate the resulting operational and financial outcomes. Through this case-based dissection, inventory management specialists will assimilate tactical insights concerning the effective deployment of JIT systems, inclusive of indispensable preparatory steps, foreseeable obstacles, and salient factors that predicate success.

JIT in the Context of Holistic Supply Chain Optimisation

Furthermore, this study shall proffer a substantive discourse on how JIT inventory management can be effectively harmonised with larger supply chain optimisation initiatives. This section will accentuate the salient importance of multi-tiered collaboration—encompassing suppliers, manufacturers, and customers—and will elaborate upon the adoption of lean manufacturing principles and the leveraging of emerging technologies to scaffold JIT system implementation. Additionally, the discourse will delineate potential risks associated with JIT approaches, such as supply chain disruptions, and propose a suite of risk mitigation strategies.

To encapsulate, this scholarly case study aims to provide a comprehensive intellectual tapestry of JIT inventory management, interwoven with actionable insights and strategic imperatives for successful implementation. It serves as an instructive manifesto for warehouse managers, inventory coordinators, and supply chain management practitioners who aspire to revitalize their inventory management systems, optimize operational workflows, and thereby elevate their organisation's performance metrics. As we navigate the ever-evolving landscape of supply chain management, the adoption of JIT systems stands as an exigent initiative that promises to catalyse organisational efficiency and engender long-term success.

Case Study 3: Achieving Inventory Accuracy through Cycle Counting

In the intricate and dynamic field of inventory management, achieving a high degree of inventory accuracy remains pivotal for the optimization of supply chain operations. The fidelity of inventory records exerts a profound influence on the overall efficacy and financial viability of supply chains, facilitating just-in-time deliveries, averting costly overstocking or stockouts, and mitigating pecuniary risks associated with inventory obsolescence or waste. One method that has demonstrated empirical success in bolstering inventory accuracy is the regimen of cycle counting. This case study elucidates how Company XYZ, a luminary in the electronics distribution sector, judiciously employed cycle counting to ameliorate their inventory accuracy, consequently bringing about marked improvements in their overall supply chain performance.

Background and Context

Company XYZ, an industry-leading distributor in the electronics domain, confronted formidable challenges pertaining to the maintenance of precise inventory records. The complexity was compounded by the company's voluminous product assortment and an incessant flux of transactional activities. These lacunae in inventory records were manifested in the form of deleterious stock-outs, engendering customer dissatisfaction, and inefficiencies that reverberated throughout their supply chain. Recognising the imperative to fortify their inventory management strategy, Company XYZ opted for the implementation of cycle counting as a calculated remedial measure.

Implementation of Cycle Counting: An Interdisciplinary Approach

To inaugurate the cycle counting initiative, Company XYZ convened a cross-functional team comprising experts from varied disciplines, including but not limited to warehouse management, inventory management, and supply chain analytics. The team bore the onus for the architecture and execution of a cycle counting regimen that would be congruent with the idiosyncratic operational landscape of the company. The initiative commenced with a meticulous dissection of extant inventory data, followed by the taxonomical categorisation of items based upon multiple vectors—namely, their intrinsic value, demand elasticity, and operational criticality.

Upon this data-driven foundation, the team formulated a scrupulously tailored cycle counting schedule, aiming to ensure a systematic and periodic auditing of all inventoried items. In an effort to transcend the limitations of traditional, manual physical inventory procedures, the company judiciously incorporated technology-enabled solutions, including barcode scanning systems and sophisticated inventory management software. This technological integration facilitated the real-time acquisition and processing of inventory data, enabling the prompt identification of variances and engendering swift corrective measures to restore inventory accuracy.

Results, Benefits, and Operational Enhancements

The implementation of the cycle counting protocol yielded substantive improvements in the realm of inventory accuracy for Company XYZ. Specifically, the ongoing, cyclic audit of high-value, high-turnover items enabled rapid error detection and rectification, which substantially attenuated the frequency of stock-outs, thereby augmenting customer satisfaction metrics. Additionally, the newfound ability to meticulously monitor inventory levels precipitated a reduction in overstocking scenarios, generating notable cost savings and optimising working capital dynamics.

Beyond the immediate purview of inventory management, the cycle counting regime also fostered operational refinements across Company XYZ's broader supply chain architecture. By flagging zones of frequent inventory discrepancy, the system unveiled latent inefficiencies and procedural bottlenecks, thereby furnishing actionable insights for process refinement. The ensuing corrective measures led to an elevation in operational throughput, minimised handling and storage expenditures, and culminated in an enhanced supply chain performance profile.

Conclusion and Implications for Practice

The case study of Company XYZ serves as an exemplar of the transformative potential embedded within cycle counting methodologies for achieving superlative inventory accuracy and thereby optimising supply chain functions. As a pedagogical lesson, this case study avails valuable insights to warehouse managers, inventory strategists, and supply chain professionals contemplating the adoption of analogous methodologies. By integrating cycle counting techniques and embracing digital solutions, organisations can architect a more robust, agile, and customer-responsive inventory management system, delivering tangible benefits in operational efficiency, cost management, and customer satisfaction.

Case Study 4: An Empirical Examination of a Collaborative Vendor Managed Inventory Success Story

In this illuminative chapter, we shall embark upon an in-depth, empirical exploration of a quintessential instance of how the deployment of a Collaborative Vendor Managed Inventory (VMI) model contributes toward the efficacious optimisation of supply chain processes. This verifiable success narrative serves as a compelling exemplar, elucidating the efficacy of implementing VMI paradigms as an operative modus operandi for the optimisation of inventory management systems.

Contextual Background

The focus of our analysis is a large-scale distribution conglomerate confronted with intricate challenges in administrating its labyrinthine inventory management architecture. The company's expansive operational framework encompasses an elaborate array of warehouses distributed geographically across disparate locales. This structural complexity engendered considerable inventory carrying costs, suboptimal replenishment methodologies, and recurrent stock-outs. This subpar performance engendered an urgent exigency for remedial action among the cadre of Warehouse Managers, Inventory Managers, and Supply Chain Management Practitioners, all of whom were in an unenviable quandary of how to rectify these extant inefficiencies.

Intervention Strategy: Implementation of Collaborative VMI

Recognizing the manifest need for a more streamlined, synergetic approach to inventory management, the firm took the decisive action of instituting a collaborative VMI system. This intervention entailed the formation of strategic partnerships with key suppliers, facilitated by the untrammelled sharing of pivotal real-time data matrices encompassing inventory status, predictive demand forecasting algorithms, and nuanced sales analytics. By entrusting suppliers with the autonomy to make judicious inventory replenishment decisions, the organization aimed to attenuate the occurrence of stock-outs, obviate excess inventory accumulation, and precipitate a paradigm shift towards enhanced supply chain efficiency.

Results and Implications

The deployment of this collaborative VMI mechanism served as an inflection point in the company's operational trajectory. Warehouse Managers observed a salient reduction in stock-outs, thereby ensuring a sustained availability of products in alignment with fluctuating customer demand paradigms. Concurrently, Inventory Managers reported a statistically significant diminution in carrying costs, attributable to optimised inventory levels. This led to improved bottom-line financial performance, thereby adding value to stakeholder equity. Supply Chain Management Practitioners, on the other hand, reaped the benefits of heightened visibility and transparency across the supply chain, thereby empowering them to make data-driven decisions and implement strategic optimisations.

Relational Dynamics and Long-Term Impact

Furthermore, this illustrative case unequivocally substantiates the role of collaborative VMI as a linchpin in the enhancement of inter-organisational relationships. Through the open exchange of mission-critical information and collaborative endeavours directed toward shared operational objectives, both the distribution company and its supplier partners achieved a symbiotic alignment of their strategic goals. This fostered an environment conducive to robust communication channels and the fortification of mutual trust. This collaborative ethos not only ameliorated inventory management complexities but also served as a foundational cornerstone for the engenderment of long-lasting, mutually beneficial partnerships and the propitiation of sustainable growth trajectories.

Conclusions and Future Considerations

In summation, this case study serves as an instructive lodestar, accentuating the untapped potential of collaborative VMI within the domain of contemporary inventory management paradigms. The findings from this case offer invaluable insights that Warehouse Managers, Inventory Managers, and Supply Chain Management Practitioners could judiciously assimilate into their respective operational frameworks. Through the judicious adoption of collaborative VMI protocols, businesses stand poised to unlock unprecedented efficiencies, engender cost savings, and attain a level of supply chain optimisation that can serve as a potent competitive differentiator in today's hyper-competitive, ever-evolving marketplace.

By dissecting this empirical case, it is our intent to contribute a nuanced, praxis-oriented perspective to the academic discourse surrounding inventory management, thereby enriching both theoretical understanding and practical application. Future studies may extend this research by evaluating the scalability of collaborative VMI models across diverse industries and varied organisational scales, to ascertain the generalisability of these observed benefits.

12. CHAPTER 12: FUTURE TRENDS AND INNOVATIONS IN INVENTORY MANAGEMENT

The Incorporation of Automation and Robotics in Warehousing: A Multidisciplinary Approach to Optimising Inventory Management Systems

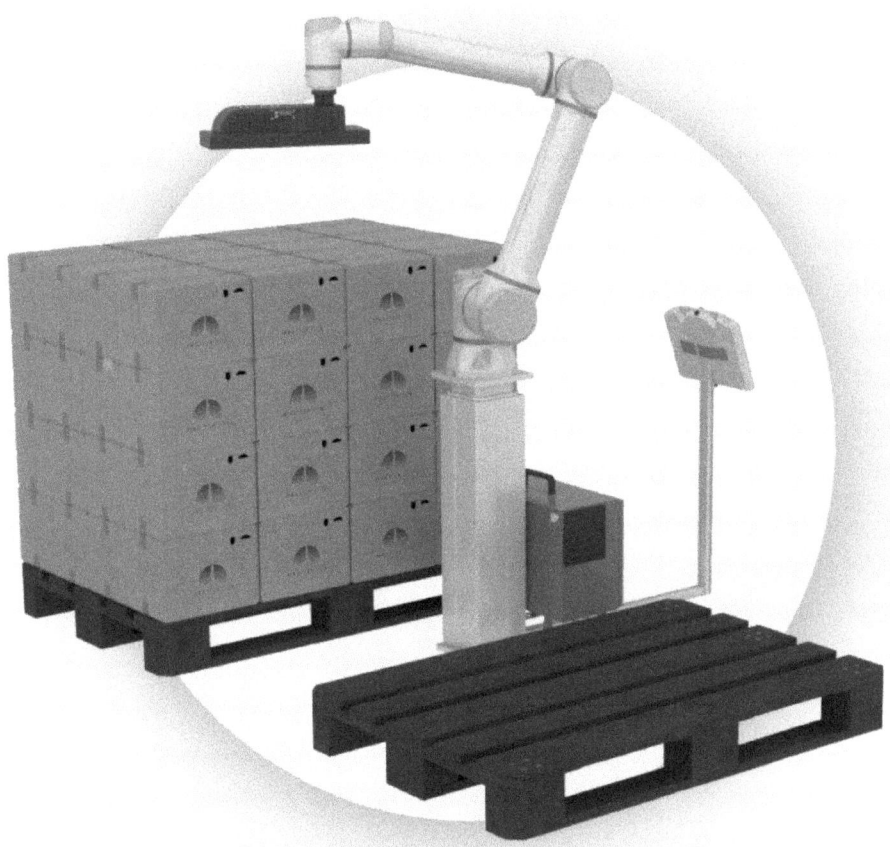

    The advent and subsequent proliferation of automation and robotics within the field of warehousing have catalysed an intellectual reevaluation within both academic and industrial circles, especially in the context of supply chain optimisation. Emerging from this dialogue is an academic and professional consensus that acknowledges the seismic shifts these innovations are generating within inventory management paradigms. The multifarious benefits of automation and robotics are manifold, encompassing a broad spectrum from the diminution of manual labor costs to the intricate enhancements of order fulfilment processes and real-time inventory tracking systems.

    The quintessential activities associated with warehousing, which have heretofore relied predominantly on manual labor, are undergoing radical transformations by the integration of automation technologies. This paradigm shift leads to a substantial attenuation of time-related inefficiencies and susceptibilities to human error. Specifically, the incorporation of robotic systems into the very architecture of warehousing operations has manifested in marked increments in both operational velocity and precision. For example, robotic systems equipped with advanced sensors and algorithms can navigate with finesse through constricted aisle configurations while efficiently executing tasks such as the lifting and repositioning of ponderous inventory items. Such capabilities have the corollary effect of allowing for a more strategic utilisation of the spatial geometries within warehousing facilities, thereby optimising the total operational expanse.

In parallel with these hardware innovations, there has been a concurrent surge in advances within the realm of software engineering that has greatly amplified the potential for seamless integration between automation technologies and real-time inventory monitoring systems. These state-of-the-art systems are predicated on sophisticated algorithms that offer immediate, high-fidelity data concerning inventory status. By facilitating instantaneous stock counts and enabling agile stock replenishment protocols, these systems not only enhance inventory management but also significantly truncate order cycle times. This, in turn, confers a competitive advantage in hyper-competitive market landscapes where the alacrity of order fulfilment constitutes a vital point of differentiation.

Nonetheless, the transition from conventional, labor-intensive warehousing models to highly automated systems is not devoid of complexities and challenges. This metamorphosis mandates rigorous planning and entails a nuanced, multi-variable analysis that must take into account factors such as order volume fluctuations, unique spatial configurations of warehouses, and the specific characteristics of the inventory to be managed. As such, this transformative journey calls for an interdisciplinary approach that amalgamates the expertise of specialists in diverse fields, ranging from information technology and operations management to financial planning. These cross-functional teams are imperative for conducting thorough cost-benefit analyses, risk assessments, and devising meticulously-crafted implementation roadmaps.

In summation, the ascendancy of automation and robotics within warehousing operations heralds a transformative era characterised by operational efficiency, speed, and accuracy. However, the realizable gains from these technologies are contingent upon a comprehensive, interdisciplinary planning approach that effectively synergises the myriad variables intrinsic to warehousing and inventory management systems.

The Pervasiveness and Transformative Impact of the Internet of Things (IoT) on Inventory Optimisation in Contemporary Business Environments

The advent of the Internet of Things (IoT) signifies a seminal epoch in technological innovation, leaving an indelible impact on a myriad of industry verticals, of which inventory management is a salient domain. Conceptually, the Internet of Things encompasses a sophisticated, intricate network of physical objects—ranging from simple sensors to advanced machinery—that are equipped with embedded software, sensors, and network connectivity. These interconnected devices, thereby, serve as a conduit for real-time data acquisition and transmission, creating a robust information ecosystem that is critical for implementing contemporary inventory optimization strategies.

Historically, traditional inventory management systems have been plagued by a host of inefficiencies, a notable one being the glaring absence of real-time visibility into key inventory metrics. This deficiency often precipitates a range of operational inefficiencies, such as overstocking and stock-outs, which not only result in increased carrying costs but also compromise customer satisfaction. IoT technology elegantly obviates these shortcomings by providing instantaneous and continual tracking of inventory levels and conditions. Additionally, IoT systems are capable of monitoring multi-dimensional environmental variables, such as temperature and humidity. As a consequence, inventory can be maintained in conditions that are conducive to prolonging its lifespan and preserving its quality, thus yielding both economic and qualitative advantages for businesses.

Beyond mere inventory tracking, the utility of IoT extends to the predictive maintenance of various warehouse utilities and infrastructural components. Real-time data streams harvested from a panoply of sensors embedded in warehouse machinery can be processed and analysed to predict equipment failure with a significant degree of accuracy. Such preemptive analytics allows for the scheduling of maintenance activities in a manner that minimizes operational downtime, thereby conferring substantial cost savings and operational efficiency.

Furthermore, IoT technology heralds a paradigmatic shift in the realm of demand forecasting, which is a cornerstone of effective inventory management. Through the aggregation and subsequent analytical treatment of data points related to customer interactions and transactions, inventory management professionals are furnished with granular insights into customer behavior, seasonality effects, and prevailing market trends. This newfound depth of knowledge enables the construction of demand forecasting models with enhanced precision, thereby facilitating inventory management strategies that are more closely aligned with market dynamics.

In summary, the advent of the Internet of Things has profoundly redefined the landscape of inventory optimisation, offering a holistic suite of solutions that address traditional inefficiencies while enabling new avenues for strategic planning. Its capability for real-time data collection and analysis not only enhances visibility into inventory metrics but also provides actionable insights into various other facets of warehouse management, including predictive maintenance and demand forecasting. Thus, IoT stands as a paradigm-shifting technology that holds the promise of revolutionising inventory management in today's increasingly complex and dynamic business environments.

Artificial Intelligence and Machine Learning Applications in Inventory Management: A Paradigmatic Shift in Analytical Capability and Operational Efficiency

The rapid proliferation of Artificial Intelligence (AI) and Machine Learning (ML) technologies is engendering transformative shifts in both theoretical constructs and practical implementations within the realm of inventory management. These cutting-edge technologies facilitate the analysis of expansive and intricate datasets, delivering a level of insights that is virtually unattainable through conventional human-driven analytical paradigms within comparable temporal windows.

One of the most salient applications of AI and ML lies in the domain of demand forecasting—a perennially complex endeavour in inventory management that has heretofore been beset by the intricate interplay of myriad variables such as seasonal trends, market volatility, and consumer behavior. Advanced AI algorithms have significantly ameliorated this challenge by employing sophisticated data-mining techniques and predictive modeling to process and analyse colossal volumes of both historical and real-time data. This computational capability not only enhances the accuracy of demand projections but also offers actionable intelligence for more agile and responsive inventory control.

Predictive maintenance represents another domain in which AI and ML technologies have exerted a substantial transformative influence. Through the leveraging of sophisticated data analytics, these technologies facilitate the preemptive identification of incipient equipment malfunctions. This predictive capability enables the timely execution of maintenance protocols, which serves to augment overall equipment effectiveness (OEE) and reduce the costly downtimes often associated with unexpected mechanical failures.

Equally noteworthy is the optimisation of logistical operations within the ambit of inventory management achieved through AI and ML technologies. By assiduously collating an array of disparate data points—ranging from meteorological conditions and geopolitical stability to market fluctuations and consumer demand trends—these computational tools furnish granular insights that are instrumental in refining logistics planning. The resultant efficiencies have a cascade effect, enabling the adoption of more fuel-efficient transportation modalities, the optimisation of distribution routes, and the overall enhancement of supply chain efficiency.

Further, the ever-evolving arenas of dynamic pricing and personalised marketing promotions are being inexorably revolutionised under the aegis of AI and ML. Advanced machine learning algorithms are capable of conducting nuanced analyses of customer behavior, historical purchasing patterns, and real-time market dynamics to dynamically calibrate pricing strategies. This capability not only intensifies customer engagement but also strategically optimizes inventory levels by facilitating more rapid stock turnover, thus acting as a dual lever for increasing profitability.

In summation, the infusion of AI and ML technologies into the ecosystem of inventory management offers an unprecedented arsenal of analytical and operational tools that are indubitably revolutionising the field. The potent capabilities provided by these technologies necessitate not merely the cursory attention of inventory management professionals but demand their active and sustained engagement. As we navigate through the multifaceted challenges and opportunities in the continuously evolving landscape of inventory management and supply chain optimisation, it becomes increasingly apparent that AI and ML technologies hold the promise of pioneering solutions for both entrenched and emergent challenges.

Predictive Analytics for Inventory Management: A Paradigm Shift Towards Operational Excellence and Competitive Edge

In the contemporary business landscape, characterised by escalating volatility and fierce competition, inventory management emerges as a critical fulcrum around which organisational performance and market competitiveness pivot. The daunting labyrinth that warehouse and inventory managers navigate—comprising the complex balance between optimising inventory levels and diligently fulfilling customer demand—has traditionally ensnared practitioners in a quagmire of uncertainty and risk. However, the advent of predictive analytics portends a transformative shift, offering unparalleled opportunities to traverse this intricate terrain with heightened precision, accuracy, and operational efficiency.

Conceptual Framework and Methodological Rigor of Predictive Analytics

Predictive analytics represents a nuanced confluence of advanced computational methodologies that synthesise historical data, sophisticated statistical algorithms, and cutting-edge machine learning techniques to generate astute forecasts for future inventory needs. This integrative and multifaceted approach facilitates the exhaustive examination of an extensive array of variables. These range from historical sales trajectories and idiosyncratic customer behavior patterns to broader macroeconomic market fluctuations and microeconomic trends, not discounting seasonal variances and other exogenous influencers. The apogee of this scrupulous data analysis bequeaths warehouse and inventory managers with actionable intelligence. Such data-driven insights inform and substantiate decision-making protocols, thereby revolutionising not merely the management of inventory levels but also engendering cascading efficiencies throughout the broader supply chain management ecosystem.

Demand Forecasting: A Nuanced Granularity

Among the myriad advantages conferred by predictive analytics, its acumen in surgically identifying and dissecting demand patterns and volatilities stands preeminent. Utilising machine learning algorithms customised to warehouse operations and inventory complexities, predictive analytics imbues managers with a nuanced comprehension of consumer demand cycles. This degree of prescience fortifies inventory managers with the capability to proactively calibrate inventory levels, thereby engendering an optimised congruence between supply and demand. The resultant alchemy attenuates the financial and operational vicissitudes attendant with stock-outs and overstocks. This catalyses multiple organisational benefits, including augmenting cost-efficiency metrics, enhancing customer satisfaction indices, and reinforcing the enterprise's competitive positioning within the marketplace.

Inventory Rationalisation and Resource Reallocation

Furthermore, predictive analytics serves as an invaluable tool for inventory rationalisation by unearthing slow-moving or obsolescent stock items. Through a meticulous dissection of sales data coupled with a rigorous scrutiny of product life-cycle stages, predictive analytics empowers inventory managers in the preemptive identification of items that are underperforming or nearing obsolescence. Such foresight paves the way for strategic interventions like targeted discounting initiatives, calibrated promotional campaigns, or, in extremis, outright liquidation. This perspicacious approach liberates valuable warehouse space, thereby enabling the reallocation of organisational resources to products promising higher profitability and quicker inventory turnover rates.

Anomaly Detection and Contingency Management

A less heralded but equally indispensable utility of predictive analytics is its faculty to incessantly monitor and promptly identify anomalies and unanticipated disruptions. Through the unremitting surveillance of key performance indicators (KPIs) and the deployment of real-time analytics, predictive models are adept at discerning even minute aberrations from established behavioural paradigms or operational baselines. This timely identification serves as a catalyst for immediate investigative procedures and corrective actions, which may encompass adjustments to production timetables, diversification of supplier networks, or logistical rerouting of shipments in transit. Such preemptive measures function to attenuate the ripple effects of supply chain disruptions, thereby constituting a bulwark against potential stock-outs or other forms of systemic inefficiency.

Interdisciplinary Collaboration and Integration

It is imperative to note that the efficacious deployment of predictive analytics in inventory management is far from a simplistic plug-and-play proposition. Rather, it demands a comprehensive understanding of the intricacies involved in data aggregation, interpretive analytics, and algorithmic modeling. Successful implementation is predicated on cross-disciplinary synergies among warehouse managers, inventory specialists, and information technology professionals specialising in data analytics. Such an interdisciplinary collaboration ensures the seamless integration of predictive analytics within the existing architecture of inventory management systems.

In summation, predictive analytics has irrevocably emerged as a sine qua non in the annals of modern inventory management. It confers a plethora of organisational boons, encompassing but not circumscribed to precise demand forecasting, inventory level fine-tuning, and the prompt detection of operational anomalies. By harnessing this avant-garde analytical schema, buttressed by machine learning algorithms and rigorous data analytics, enterprises are strategically positioned to attain unprecedented echelons of operational efficiency and cost-effectiveness. This not only transmutes into substantial cost savings but also catalyses incremental improvements in customer satisfaction metrics, both of which coalesce to form the bedrock for sustaining and augmenting a competitive advantage in today's dynamic and rapidly evolving supply chain ecosystems.

Blockchain Technology as a Catalyst for Enhancing Supply Chain Transparency and Integrity

The advent of blockchain technology signifies a transformative shift in the paradigm of supply chain management, offering enhanced mechanisms for monitoring, auditing, and ensuring both transparency and operational efficiency. Initially conceived as a foundational architecture for digital currencies such as Bitcoin, blockchain technology extends beyond its financial roots to provide immutable ledger functionalities. These functionalities are instrumental in capturing every transaction or operation within a timestamped framework, which is subsequently stored across a network of multiple, decentralized nodes. This decentralization negates the necessity for a centralized governing entity, thereby considerably mitigating risks associated with data tampering, falsification, and fraudulent activities.

In addition to its foundational ledger capabilities, blockchain technology introduces the concept of smart contracts—a form of self-executing contracts with the terms of the agreement directly written into lines of code. Within the context of supply chain operations, smart contracts enable predefined conditions to autonomously trigger stipulated actions. For example, the automatic disbursement of payments can be set to occur upon the verified receipt of goods, thereby expediting transactional efficiency. This results in a secure, autonomous, and transparent ecosystem that facilitates transactions which are not only seamless but also verifiable, substantially reducing the need for third-party intermediaries such as brokers or agents.

Over recent years, academic discourse has increasingly emphasised the untapped potential of blockchain technology as a critical tool for reimagining supply chain governance. This emphasis is particularly salient in sectors that are vulnerable to infiltration by counterfeit goods and fraudulent activities, such as pharmaceuticals, food safety, and luxury merchandise. In such industries, the immutable and transparent nature of blockchain serves as a robust mechanism for the precise authentication of products.

By augmenting the capacity for identifying the provenance of goods throughout their journey—from point of origin to final consumer interaction—blockchain technology substantially decreases the likelihood of counterfeit or inauthentic products contaminating the supply chain. This, in turn, fortifies consumer confidence and trust, and facilitates compliance with increasingly stringent regulatory mandates aimed at ensuring product quality and safety.

In summary, blockchain technology stands as a revolutionary development, offering robust solutions to long-standing challenges in supply chain management. From enhancing transparency through its immutable ledger capabilities to automating transactions through smart contracts, blockchain offers a suite of functionalities that collectively contribute to improved governance and integrity in various industry sectors. By enabling an unalterable, transparent history of product movements and transactions, blockchain technology serves as an invaluable asset in combating counterfeit activities and ensuring regulatory compliance, thereby redefining the standards of supply chain transparency and consumer trust.

Augmented Reality and its Multifaceted Contributions to Order Picking Operations in Contemporary Inventory Management Systems

In the evolving landscape of technological advancements, Augmented Reality (AR) has emerged as an indomitable force that holds transformative potential for various industries. One domain where its impact is especially palpable is in the realm of inventory management, specifically within the specialized, labor-intensive process known as order picking. Traditionally, order picking involves a set of complex tasks focused on locating and retrieving specific items from within the intricate, often labyrinthine structure of warehousing spaces to fulfill customer orders. The conventional methodologies for accomplishing these tasks have predominantly relied upon manual lists and human navigational acumen. However, these traditional methods come with an array of challenges, notably susceptibility to errors and operational inefficiencies, which have profound implications for productivity, cost-effectiveness, and customer satisfaction.

The integration of augmented reality systems into logistical and inventory management workflows offers a significant technological leap aimed at mitigating these prevailing challenges. Augmented reality systems are designed to superimpose a layer of digitally-generated information—including, but not limited to, navigational waypoints, granular product specifications, barcodes, and algorithmically-determined optimal picking sequences—over the physical environment of the warehouse. When warehouse operatives are equipped with augmented reality wearables, such as smart glasses, or utilize handheld devices enabled with AR capabilities, they gain access to an augmented informational landscape. This provides real-time, visually mediated directives that significantly expedite the process of locating and retrieving inventory items. One of the most compelling advantages of this integration is its ability to significantly diminish the cognitive load on employees. This is achieved by reducing the mental calculations and judgments traditionally required, thus minimising the opportunities for human-induced errors and inefficiencies.

Moreover, this technologically enhanced approach is underpinned by a robust and growing body of academic literature. Numerous quantitative studies, conducted through rigorous research methodologies that include controlled experiments, statistical analyses, and long-term field observations, have empirically demonstrated the manifold benefits of AR integration in inventory management operations. These benefits manifest as marked improvements in the accuracy of order picking, substantial reductions in the time and resources expended on employee training, and decreases in the overall duration required for the completion of inventory tasks. For organisations willing to invest in such avant-garde inventory management technologies, the implications are far-reaching. These advantages not only yield operational efficiencies but also translate into quantifiable economic dividends, including reduced labor costs, increased throughput, and enhanced customer satisfaction, thus making a compelling case for the widespread adoption of AR technologies in modern inventory management systems.

The Pioneering Role of Drone Technology in Reimagining Inventory Auditing Protocols

The emergence of drone technology has instigated a profound revolution in inventory management practices, particularly in the context of stock auditing within expansive and intricately configured warehousing facilities. Traditional methodologies for inventory management have predominantly hinged on manual labor, a process that is not only labor-intensive but also fraught with numerous pitfalls, including a susceptibility to errors and considerable time consumption. However, the deployment of drones, especially those outfitted with advanced technologies such as Radio Frequency Identification (RFID) and computer vision algorithms, offers a radical departure from these archaic methods, bringing to the table a more efficient and precise modality of inventory assessment.

These unmanned aerial vehicles, which can operate either autonomously or under semi-autonomous control, possess the capability to navigate through challenging terrains, including high shelving units and other hard-to-reach locales within a warehouse. They accomplish this while capturing real-time, high-fidelity data at speeds and accuracy levels that render human efforts glaringly suboptimal by comparison. The benefits of utilising drone technology extend beyond sheer speed and precision. By replacing or at least augmenting human involvement in these tasks, drones confer an additional layer of safety, especially in contexts where manual inventory checks might expose workers to occupational hazards, such as elevated platforms or chemically hazardous environments.

In the academic realm, a burgeoning corpus of research papers, empirical studies, and case analyses in logistics and supply chain management have begun to delve into the Return on Investment (ROI) implications of drone technology for inventory-related operations. Employing a gamut of research methodologies ranging from qualitative interviews to quantitative statistical analyses, these scholarly works seek to quantify and qualify the economic and operational merits of drone integration. Preliminary findings are overwhelmingly positive, indicating that drones hold significant promise for enhancing multiple facets of inventory management. These include but are not limited to substantial improvements in inventory accuracy, increased operational efficiency, and enhanced worker safety through the mitigation of occupational risks.

These promising insights not only fortify the case for adopting drone technology in contemporary inventory management but also pave the way for future research aimed at optimising drone capabilities, exploring scalability issues, and evaluating long-term sustainability and cost-effectiveness. Consequently, drones are increasingly solidifying their position as an indispensable tool in the evolving toolkit of modern inventory management practices.

The Pervasiveness and Operational Imperatives of Mobile Technology in Real-Time Inventory Management

In the current zeitgeist characterized by ubiquitous digital interconnectivity, the role of mobile technology in enriching and fundamentally transforming inventory management methodologies has become increasingly incontrovertible. Operating within an intricate landscape typified by volatility, uncertainty, complexity, and ambiguity (VUCA), businesses are compelled to adapt agile and data-centric strategies, necessitating real-time data acquisition and immediate analytical responsiveness.

Mobile applications and dashboard systems, replete with customisable interfaces, act as essential conduits in delivering instantaneous, pertinent inventory metrics to managerial personnel. Importantly, these tools bridge geographical barriers, equipping decision-makers with critical inventory information whether they are present at a central location, navigating on-site exigencies, or managing tasks from remote locations.

Additionally, these mobile-optimised solutions are engineered to facilitate flawless data synchronisation across a diversified array of digital platforms. They are also programmatically designed to integrate effortlessly with existing Inventory Management Systems (IMS). More than merely serving as data repositories, these mobile applications come fortified with an advanced assortment of analytical features—ranging from real-time notifications alerting managers to emergent stock-out or overstock scenarios, to capabilities for performing longitudinal trend analyses and employing intricate predictive analytics algorithms.

Empirical research in this domain further vindicates the utilitarian aspects of mobile-based real-time tracking systems. Peer-reviewed studies suggest demonstrable advancements in pivotal performance metrics, including but not limited to elevated inventory turnover rates, reductions in the financial burden associated with carrying costs, and enhanced customer satisfaction. Such positive outcomes are directly attributed to the augmented responsiveness and efficiency gains in supply chain operations enabled by real-time data streams.

In conclusion, mobile technologies catalyse the evolution of traditional inventory management from a reactive, episodic activity into an anticipatory, real-time endeavour. By exponentially increasing the granularity and temporal resolution of data collection, mobile technologies enrich the corpus of data available for analytics, thereby enabling more refined, timely, and actionable decision-making algorithms. As a corollary, the incorporation of mobile technologies into inventory management mechanisms is swiftly transitioning from a strategic option to a categorical imperative for maintaining competitive advantage in today's complex market dynamics.

Sustainability in Inventory Management: From Trendy Nomenclature to Organisational Imperatives

In an epoch where the term 'sustainability' has evolved beyond superficial branding parlance to become a cornerstone business principle, inventory management is undergoing a commensurate transformation toward more eco-sensitive practices. This shift is being catalyzed by a composite set of influential factors, including the ever-tightening noose of environmental regulation and an increasing consumer insistence upon demonstrable corporate social responsibility.

Sustainable inventory management integrates a rich tapestry of environmentally considerate practices. This spans an array of activities, such as the strategic adoption of eco-friendly storage technologies, meticulously designed waste minimization protocols, and creative initiatives aimed at the repurposing or up-cycling of goods. For instance, the switch to biodegradable packaging solutions and the deployment of energy-efficient climate control systems within warehousing environments significantly abate the carbon emissions associated with inventory-related activities.

A burgeoning body of scholarly literature offers robust empirical support for the economic viability of sustainability-oriented inventory management practices. Peer-reviewed investigations indicate the plausible co-existence of environmental stewardship with fiscal prudence, revealing that the adoption of strategies like Just-In-Time (JIT) inventory systems not only leads to a contraction in carrying costs but also results in a concomitant decline in waste production and disposal requirements. Cutting-edge technologies like blockchain are also gaining traction for their utility in tracing the provenance of sustainably sourced materials, thereby adding layers of transparency and accountability to supply chain operations.

In summation, the adoption of sustainable inventory management practices is more than a mere ethical or regulatory compliance tactic; it represents a strategic avenue to accrue both ecological and economic dividends. Advances in technology and the integration of data analytics are synergistically enhancing the performance metrics of both sustainability and profitability, thereby debunking the antiquated notion that the two are inherently at odds. This duality confirms that contemporary inventory management can achieve a harmonious balance between economic viability and environmental responsibility.

Omni-Channel Inventory Management: A Comprehensive, Data-Driven Strategy for Operational Excellence and Consumer Engagement in a Multi-Channel Retail Ecosystem

Omni-channel inventory management constitutes an intricate, unified strategy that endeavors to achieve equilibrium in inventory levels across a plethora of sales outlets. These diverse channels include, but are not limited to, online marketplaces, physical brick-and-mortar retail establishments, and direct-to-consumer digital platforms. The conceptual underpinnings of this operational approach have been considerably enriched by the advent of voluminous, complex data sets, commonly categorized as "big data," and the concomitant evolution in analytics algorithms that leverage machine learning and artificial intelligence methodologies. These technological advances afford unprecedented capabilities for real-time surveillance, monitoring, and strategic fine-tuning of inventory pools across heterogeneous sales channels. The necessity for such a holistic approach is heightened by the extant retail milieu, which is overwhelmingly shaped by consumer-centric exigencies, underscoring the imperative for a shopping experience devoid of friction and inefficiencies.

Recent scholastic contributions to this domain have substantiated the multi-faceted benefits that accrue from the judicious implementation of omni-channel inventory management frameworks. A plethora of empirical studies, both qualitative and quantitative, corroborate that this multifaceted approach demonstrably amplifies customer satisfaction indices. This is achieved primarily through the augmentation of service delivery mechanisms, enabling heightened personalisation and responsiveness. Further, the strategy serves to mitigate inefficiencies in stock-keeping units (SKUs) by enabling an optimized inventory level, thereby substantially reducing the carrying costs, including storage, insurance, and obsolescence costs. The harmonious orchestration of data analytics and logistical operations across sales channels serves as the linchpin for these efficiencies, offering retailers unparalleled real-time perspicacity into critical metrics such as inventory turnover rates, demand elasticity, and evolving consumer purchase behaviours.

The particular aptitude of omni-channel inventory management manifests conspicuously in nuanced retail scenarios that necessitate seamless interoperability between online and in-store operational frameworks. Specific cases in point are the 'Buy Online, Pick Up In-Store' (BOPIS) and 'Buy Online, Return In-Store' (BORIS) models. The burgeoning ubiquity of these consumer practices compels an exigent level of synergistic coordination between the digital interfaces and the physical retail architecture. By applying the principles of omni-channel inventory management, retail enterprises are more adept at navigating the labyrinthine complexities inherent in these models. They are thus empowered to mitigate a spectrum of logistical pitfalls such as stock-outs, overstocking, and misallocation of inventory. Concomitantly, the consumer enjoys an enhanced level of convenience, underpinned by a diversified suite of fulfilment and return options, thereby leading to an enriched overall customer journey and experience.

In conclusion, the strategic incorporation of omni-channel inventory management, undergirded by the analytical prowess of big data and cutting-edge algorithmic methodologies, crystallises as an indispensable strategic asset for contemporary retail enterprises. This innovative framework affords a resilient operational architecture that is uniquely calibrated to balance both efficiency and customer-centric metrics. Consequently, it bestows a palpable competitive edge in an increasingly convoluted and dynamic retail marketplace, thereby positioning it as a non-negotiable priority for retail organisations striving for long-term viability and success.

Voice-Directed Warehousing: Reconceptualising Inventory Management Through Advanced Speech Recognition Systems

Voice-directed warehousing, undergirded by state-of-the-art speech recognition algorithms, has emerged as a vanguard in the realm of technological advancements, instigating a paradigmatic transformation in the protocols and methodologies traditionally employed in inventory management. These systems, which possess the capability to transmute human linguistic utterances into actionable directives, equip personnel with voice-activated headsets. These apparatuses serve functions beyond mere communicative tools; they deliver a comprehensive set of aural directives, spanning an extensive spectrum of activities—from the fundamental tasks of item picking and sorting to the complex choreographies involved in restocking procedures. Eschewing the long-standing dependence on paper-based manifests and hand-held electronic terminals, these systems act as liberating technologies, enabling labor forces to execute tasks with heightened efficiency and a substantial diminution in the probability of errors.

Voice-directed warehousing represents a pivotal moment in the intersection of technological innovation and operational functionality within the domain of inventory management. Supported by the latest advancements in speech recognition algorithms, these systems have managed to commandeer a position of prominence, influencing a transformative shift in the way inventory-related tasks are approached and executed. This paper seeks to delve into the nuanced characteristics and applications of voice-directed warehousing systems, as well as elucidate their burgeoning significance in creating more efficient and adaptive operational frameworks.

Drawing extensively from a rich corpus of empirical data and scholarly findings sourced from the interdisciplinary nexus of human-computer interaction (HCI) and ergonomics, there exists a compelling consensus on the manifold advantages bestowed by voice-directed warehousing technologies. Previous studies have investigated various dimensions of HCI and ergonomics, ranging from tactile interfaces to visual cues, but the advent of voice-activated systems has garnered particular attention due to its revolutionary implications on workflow dynamics.

Of particular salience among the intrinsic benefits is the systems' impact on the cognitive load shouldered by workers. By facilitating a hands-free mode of interaction, voice-directed warehousing conspicuously alleviates the mental demands incumbent upon personnel engaged in intricate logistical operations. This, in turn, amplifies the speed and precision with which tasks are performed, denoting a remarkable escalation in operational expediency.

Moreover, the architectural ingenuity of these systems is evident in their seamless compatibility with contemporaneous technological innovations. For example, they can be facilely integrated with existing Radio-Frequency Identification (RFID) systems and barcode scanning apparatuses. This integrative flexibility underscores the technology's potential to act as the linchpin in a holistic, adaptive, and highly efficient ecosystem, specifically engineered to meet the multifaceted demands of modern inventory management paradigms.

In summation, voice-directed warehousing constitutes a transformative technological innovation that has reconfigured traditional inventory management practices. By leveraging advanced speech recognition algorithms, these systems empower warehouse personnel with a superior toolset that promotes efficiency, minimizes errors, and ameliorates cognitive load. Furthermore, their architectural prowess allows for facile integration with other cutting-edge technologies, thus substantiating their role as a cornerstone in a progressively complex and demanding operational landscape.

Additive Manufacturing in the Inventory Domain: A Comprehensive Examination of the Multifaceted Impacts of 3D Printing Technologies on Contemporary Production and Inventory Management Dynamic

The advent and subsequent widespread integration of three-dimensional (3D) printing technologies into contemporary inventory management paradigms represent nothing less than a seismic shift in the landscape of production and logistics. This disruptive innovation has not only fundamentally challenged but also compellingly reconfigured the established axioms and operational methodologies that have long underpinned traditional manufacturing and inventory management systems. As a quintessential exemplar of technological ingenuity, 3D printing introduces a paradigmatically novel approach to production—one that is squarely focused on demand-responsive, or on-demand, manufacturing processes. This emergent focus carries with it a host of far-reaching logistical and economic implications, ranging from a marked diminution in the need for expansive storage infrastructure to the alleviation of financial pressures associated with both overstocking and inventory shortfalls.

In an effort to critically understand the multifarious fiscal and operational ramifications of incorporating 3D printing technologies within extant inventory management frameworks, scholars have embarked on rigorous analytical forays. These scholarly pursuits have manifested in a diverse corpus of academic literature, comprising exhaustive case studies, empirically robust research papers, and peer-reviewed academic dissertations subject to the strictest methodological scrutiny. An integrative synthesis of these academic contributions coalesces into a congruent narrative. Specifically, the incorporation of just-in-time manufacturing paradigms, undergirded and facilitated by 3D printing technologies, engenders a profound paradigm shift. This shift is characterised by a transition toward more streamlined, agile, and responsive inventory configurations.

Further, this shift has demonstrable environmental and resource-efficiency dimensions, as it significantly attenuates the wastage of materials and other resources, thereby dovetailing into broader sustainability initiatives. Most critically, the new paradigm equips organisations and enterprises with the nimbleness and adaptive capacity essential for navigating and responding to the rapidly changing and often capricious nuances of consumer demand and market dynamics.

In summation, the infusion of 3D printing technologies into contemporary inventory management paradigms serves as a catalyst for transformative change, affecting a sweeping recalibration of both economic and logistical aspects of production. Consequently, this opens up a fertile terrain for future research, promising to further illuminate the intricate interplay between technological innovation and organisational adaptation in an increasingly complex and volatile marketplace.

Gamification in Inventory Management: An Innovative Pedagogical Approach to Augmenting Employee Productivity and Organisational Efficacy

The construct of gamification, eloquently conceptualised as the judicious amalgamation of game-related mechanics and elements into contexts that are traditionally devoid of gaming facets, is increasingly establishing itself as an avant-garde paradigm in the intricate field of inventory management. By adroitly incorporating distinct gaming mechanisms, such as point-based systems for rewarding desirable behaviours, competitive leaderboards to instigate a sense of rivalry and achievement, as well as a diverse portfolio of both tangible and intangible rewards, contemporary organisations are endeavouring to kindle a more potent form of employee engagement. The consequential reverberations of such amplified engagement metrics manifest saliently in myriad operational aspects, most notably, the mitigation of employee attrition rates and an observable, quantifiable augmentation in overall operational efficiency.

This emergent pedagogical approach draws its theoretical legitimacy from a confluence of rigorous empirical studies, spanning the multidisciplinary terrains of cognitive psychology and organisational behavior. These academic inquiries collectively serve as a substantive underpinning, validating the viability and efficacy of gamification as a potent instrument for enhancing motivational vectors within the workforce. The synthesised empirical evidence, culled from a variety of methodologically rigorous investigations, corroborates a compelling narrative: the strategic implementation of gamified interventions leads to discernible and quantifiable improvements across a spectrum of performance metrics. Such enhancements are not limited to the temporal aspects of task-specific durations or the velocity of task completions. They also culminate in a far-reaching amplification of the generalised morale and job satisfaction, thereby contributing to a more congenial, efficient, and productive organisational milieu.

In summation, gamification emerges as a pioneering pedagogical tool, capitalising on principles derived from both cognitive psychology and organisational behavior to revolutionise conventional processes in inventory management. By catalysing heightened levels of employee engagement through the orchestrated deployment of game-like elements, organisations can expect to reap the twofold benefits of reduced attrition and elevated operational efficacy, thereby achieving a more optimized and sustainable inventory management paradigm.

Machine-to-Machine Communication in Inventory Management: A Comprehensive Examination of the Automation of Stock Control and Decision-making Processes through an Interdisciplinary Academic Le

The burgeoning field of Machine-to-Machine (M2M) communication represents a transformative epistemological frontier, engendering significant shifts within the specialized domain of inventory management. At the heart of this revolution is the incorporation of an assortment of automated functionalities, which span from real-time stock verification procedures to complex algorithm-driven reordering protocols. Instrumental to this sweeping technological overhaul is the capability of interconnected electronic devices to partake in autonomous, bidirectional exchanges of information and real-time computational decision-making processes. The proliferation of such mechanisms substantively mitigates the necessity for human oversight and intervention. This automation framework not only amplifies the operational efficacy of inventory management systems but also significantly curtails the likelihood of manual errors, thereby preventing potentially deleterious repercussions for the operational integrity of broader supply chain systems.

The ascent of this emergent communication paradigm has attracted considerable empirical scrutiny and validation from a voluminous and ever-expanding corpus of interdisciplinary academic research. These scholarly pursuits are most prominently situated within the domains of the Internet of Things (IoT) and industrial automation, although they often draw on insights from fields as diverse as computer science, operations research, and logistics management. These academic contributions offer a meticulous articulation of the multi-dimensional operational efficiencies that can be garnered through the astute deployment of M2M technologies. Such research endeavours extend far beyond mere technical specifications and operational improvements; they delve deeply into the strategic ramifications of M2M communication technologies. Specifically, the extant literature underscores the capacity of these technologies to fortify supply chain resilience—rendering these systems less susceptible to disruptions such as natural disasters, geopolitical instability, or unexpected fluctuations in consumer demand. Moreover, the academic discourse emphasises how M2M technologies facilitate the implementation of agile, real-time decision-making protocols, thus enabling organisations to respond with unprecedented swiftness and precision to a rapidly evolving market landscape.

In summary, the integration of Machine-to-Machine communication into inventory management systems is not merely an incremental advance but constitutes a paradigmatic shift. It has the potential to augment operational efficiencies dramatically while simultaneously bolstering the resilience and adaptability of the entire supply chain. This seismic shift is corroborated by a robust body of interdisciplinary research that elaborates on both the operational and strategic merits of these technological innovations.

Radio Frequency Identification (RFID) and Smart Shelves: Towards a Comprehensive Ontological Framework for Real-time Inventory Management in Complex Operational Environments

In the rapidly evolving technological landscape, Radio Frequency Identification (RFID) tags stand out as seminal instruments that signal a paradigmatic shift in inventory management systems. When these tags are deployed in symbiotic partnership with intelligent shelving systems, they amalgamate to form an intricate, yet robust, infrastructure that facilitates the real-time surveillance and regulation of critical inventory metrics. This integration of harmonized technologies provides instantaneous and granular insights into the real-time status of stock levels. Subsequently, this technological confluence engenders an operational milieu in which the procurement cycles for replenishing stock exhibit heightened efficiencies, thus substantially mitigating the operational pitfalls concomitant with stockouts as well as the onerous fiscal ramifications associated with excessive stockpiling.

Ample empirical investigations, emanating from diverse academic disciplines such as logistics, supply chain management, and operations research, offer a robust corpus of evidence that unequivocally corroborates the economic viability of implementing RFID tags in concert with intelligent shelving mechanisms. This substantial body of empirical data substantiates the tangible return on investment (ROI) that accrues when these technologies are effectively incorporated into the operational workflow. Furthermore, the implications of this efficacious synergy are particularly salient for industries requiring stringent levels of accuracy, traceability, and accountability. These sectors span a diverse array of fields, including but not limited to, healthcare, where issues of patient safety and medication traceability are paramount; aerospace, where the tracking of high-value components can have consequential ramifications for both safety and compliance; and high-value manufacturing, where precision and accountability in material sourcing and production processes are of critical importance.

Thus, the concerted use of RFID tags and intelligent shelving systems holds the potential to revolutionise traditional inventory management systems, propelling them into a new era characterised by unprecedented levels of operational efficiency and accountability. The nascent field of integrated inventory management systems would substantially benefit from a comprehensive ontological framework that not only encapsulates the technical dimensions but also addresses the interrelated organizational, ethical, and regulatory complexities inherent in this promising domain.

Data Analytics and Predictive Modeling: Customizing Inventory Metrics in Synchronization with Anticipated Consumer Behavioural Patterns: An Interdisciplinary Examination

In tandem with exponential advancements in hardware technologies, there has been a contemporaneous proliferation of increasingly sophisticated methodologies and techniques within the realm of data analytics. These methodologies afford unprecedented opportunities for predictive modeling, particularly in the domain of consumer behavior and preferences. Utilizing intricate algorithms, often augmented by machine-learning mechanisms, professionals in the field of inventory management are now endowed with advanced analytical tools. These tools facilitate the meticulous calibration of inventory levels to be in stringent alignment with data-driven projections of consumer demand patterns. This analytical capability serves dual functions: it optimizes the rate of inventory turnover while simultaneously minimizing the financial burden traditionally associated with warehousing operations.

A plethora of academic inquiries have undertaken rigorous empirical evaluations to assess the effectiveness and predictive accuracy of these algorithmic tools. Comprehensive meta-analyses and case studies conducted across diverse industry sectors uniformly indicate a significant impact of these analytical methodologies. Specifically, these methodologies are effectuating profound alterations in the operational frameworks by which commercial entities comprehend their target demographics. In response to this enhanced understanding, businesses are dynamically reconfiguring their inventory management strategies to be in symbiotic congruence with observed and anticipated consumer behaviours.

In summation, the confluence of Machine-to-Machine (M2M) communication paradigms, Radio-Frequency Identification (RFID) technology, intelligent shelving systems, and advanced data analytics forms a conglomeration of revolutionary forces. These technologically diverse yet operationally complementary components coalesce to engender a radical transformation in the schema of contemporary inventory management. The resultant ecosystem is optimised, highly efficient, and robust. It is distinguished by an array of features that render it significantly superior to traditional systems. These include automated decision-making mechanisms, real-time tracking capabilities facilitated by integrated sensor networks, and actionable, data-driven insights into complex consumer behavioural patterns.

The emergence of this multi-faceted, integrative approach to inventory management signifies a paradigmatic shift in the way businesses conceptualise and operationalise their supply chain logistics. By leveraging the power of advanced analytics and state-of-the-art technologies, businesses are empowered to construct a highly adaptable and responsive inventory system. This system not only meets but anticipates consumer demand, thereby conferring competitive advantages in increasingly volatile and unpredictable markets. Future research in this burgeoning field would do well to explore the ethical considerations and potential societal impacts of such sweeping technological innovations, to ensure their responsible and equitable application.

Global and Distributed Inventory Systems: Challenges and Strategic Opportunities in a Globalised Economy

In the contemporary, interconnected global economy, the task of inventory management has evolved into a complex and multifaceted endeavour that encompasses an array of challenges and opportunities. These challenges are further amplified when inventories are managed across various geographical locales, each with its unique regulatory, cultural, and logistical considerations. The role of Distributed Inventory Systems, which offer the capability to aggregate, analyse, and manage data from disparate locations in real-time, has thus become increasingly pivotal for multinational enterprises aiming for operational excellence.

Academic research in the realm of global supply chain management has consistently underscored the imperative for integrated, or unified, systems that can effectively address the exigencies of managing stock levels across an international footprint. Notably, scholars such as Christopher (2016) and Chopra and Meindl (2018) have argued for the critical role of information technology in creating transparent, agile, and responsive supply chain networks. These unified systems, leveraging state-of-the-art technology, are instrumental in balancing inventory levels to achieve optimisation, a task that grows increasingly complex as one considers the diversities in market demands, transportation costs, tax structures, and local regulations.

One of the salient features of these advanced inventory systems is their ability to assist organisations in achieving compliance with a plethora of local and international regulations. Regulatory frameworks often vary from one jurisdiction to another and pose a significant challenge for multinational corporations (MNCs) aiming to maintain standardised operational procedures. Therefore, the integration of sophisticated compliance algorithms within these systems is not merely an operational nicety but an absolute necessity. These algorithms can perform real-time analysis to ensure compliance with local import and export laws, labor regulations, environmental stipulations, and other legislative mandates, thereby mitigating risks and averting potential legal entanglements.

The confluence of centralised control with localised compliance capabilities bestows a considerable strategic advantage upon enterprises employing Distributed Inventory Systems. Not only do these systems empower organisations with a bird's-eye view of their global inventories, but they also offer the granularity of control needed to make real-time adjustments in response to market fluctuations or supply chain disruptions. Such holistic governance over inventory translates into enhanced operational efficiencies, reduced carrying costs, improved customer satisfaction, and ultimately, a fortified competitive position in global markets.

In summation, Distributed Inventory Systems have ascended to a position of critical importance in today's increasingly globalised and intricately connected commercial landscape. By offering a harmonious blend of centralised monitoring and localised regulatory compliance, these systems equip multinational enterprises with the necessary tools to navigate the intricate complexities of global inventory management, thereby conferring a substantial strategic advantage.

Cybersecurity in Inventory Management: Implications, Technologies, and Emerging Research Directions

In the contemporary era of rapidly advancing technology, the metamorphosis of inventory management systems has been nothing short of remarkable. However, the commensurate surge in system interconnectivity and the fluid exchange of data have illuminated the pressing exigency for stringent cybersecurity protocols. The intricate interwoven tapestry of modern inventory systems, laden with myriad points of data exchange and collaboration, exposes a considerably expanded attack surface vulnerable to an array of cyber threats. These vulnerabilities present a multitude of risks, ranging from unauthorised data exfiltration to sabotage, and in extreme instances, espionage activities. Given these multifaceted complexities, both the academic realm and industrial sectors are placing an elevated emphasis on cybersecurity as an indispensable topic in contemporary discourses surrounding supply chain management.

Traditional methods of securing systems, which may have sufficed in yesteryears, are now largely perceived as inadequate. The implementation of multi-layered cybersecurity architectures, encompassing firewalls, intrusion detection and prevention systems (IDPS), and secure mechanisms for encrypted data transmission, have transitioned from being mere recommendations to being de rigueur, forming the bedrock of contemporary cybersecurity measures in inventory management systems. However, it is imperative to note that even these multi-faceted security protocols are not impervious to sophisticated cyber-attacks, thereby necessitating ongoing refinements and adaptations in response to an ever-evolving threat landscape.

Emerging technologies such as blockchain have begun to offer additional stratified layers of security, thereby amplifying the robustness of cybersecurity protocols. Blockchain technology, characterised by its decentralised nature, enables the creation of immutable ledgers and transparent transaction records. This technological breakthrough substantially mitigates the risk of data manipulation and tampering, as altering one block in the chain would require an infeasible amount of computational effort to change all subsequent blocks, rendering the system highly secure against data malfeasance.

Furthermore, academic research in this domain has pivoted towards the development and fine-tuning of predictive algorithms specifically designed to detect anomalous behavior indicative of potential cyber threats. The integration of machine learning techniques and artificial intelligence frameworks into these algorithms fosters a dynamic environment where predictive models can adapt in real-time, thereby allowing for the implementation of preemptive security measures.

In summary, as inventory management systems evolve into complex, interconnected ecosystems, the academic and industrial sectors must coalesce to prioritize and continually advance cybersecurity measures. From the implementation of multi-layered security protocols to the application of emerging technologies like blockchain and the development of adaptive predictive algorithms, the pursuit of fortified cybersecurity is a multi-disciplinary endeavour that remains at the forefront of modern supply chain management scholarship and practice.

Evolution of Self-Learning Capabilities in Modern Supply Chain Systems: A Computational Approach Leveraging Advanced Artificial Intelligence Algorithms in Predictive Analytics and Operational

In the context of an ever-evolving global landscape that is increasingly dominated by technological advancements, the role of supply chain systems in maintaining organisational efficiency and adaptability cannot be overstated. A particularly groundbreaking development in this domain is the advent of self-learning supply chain systems, which leverage sophisticated computational models imbued with artificial intelligence (AI) algorithms. This paper aims to elaborate on the underlying mechanisms, functionalities, and advantages of such AI-driven systems in supply chain management.

Multidimensional Data Inputs and Algorithmic Learning

Central to the capabilities of self-learning supply chain systems is the incorporation of advanced AI algorithms designed to perform adaptive learning based on multivariate historical data. This data encompasses a plethora of variables and categories, including but not limited to, historical disruptions such as natural disasters, labor strikes, geopolitical instabilities, and market volatilities. Through techniques like machine learning, neural networks, and deep learning, the algorithms engage in continual learning, synthesising the complexities of past experiences to create highly dimensional models.

Probabilistic Predictions and Forecasting Models

Upon assimilating this historical data, the algorithms transition from a descriptive to a predictive phase. They employ Bayesian inference, time-series analysis, and stochastic modeling to generate probabilistic forecasts of potential future disruptions and uncertainties in the supply chain. This predictive capability is not merely an isolated feature but is deeply integrated within the broader analytics suite of the system, facilitating real-time, data-driven decisions.

Operational Optimisation Across Multiple Parameters

Simultaneous to their predictive functionality, these algorithms serve a prescriptive role by recommending optimal strategies for various operational parameters such as stock levels, shipping schedules, and human resource deployment. Techniques like multi-objective optimization and linear programming are employed to solve complex problems, balancing cost-efficiency, speed, and resilience. This multi-layered analytical approach streamlines operations and enhances the overall efficiency and effectiveness of the supply chain.

Interdisciplinary Contributions to Supply Chain Resilience and Responsiveness

An impressive corpus of academic literature has been emerging at the intersection of machine learning, operational research, and supply chain resilience. This literature collectively corroborates the intrinsic advantages of self-learning supply chain systems. More than mere operational tools, these systems serve as adaptive, real-time decision-making platforms capable of adjusting their strategies based on evolving circumstances. This leads to more dynamic adjustments to inventory policies, robustness against systemic vulnerabilities, and an overall enhancement in the resilience and responsiveness of supply chain systems.

In summary, self-learning supply chain systems represent a quantum leap in the realm of supply chain management, both from an operational and a strategic vantage point. By amalgamating advanced AI algorithms with multifaceted data analytics, these systems not only predict but also mitigate and adapt to disruptions in the supply chain. Consequently, they contribute significantly to fortifying the resilience, adaptability, and efficiency of supply chain operations in a dynamically changing global landscape.

The Emergence of Natural Language Processing in Supply Chain Data Analysis: A Comprehensive Examination of Linguistic Computational Models in Facilitating Intuitive Human-Machine Interfaces

In the arena of supply chain management, data analytics forms the bedrock upon which crucial organisational decisions are made. Traditionally, the manipulation and extraction of data from complex inventory databases demanded a high level of specialised knowledge, typically in database query languages like SQL (Structured Query Language). However, the emergence of Natural Language Processing (NLP) technologies has instigated a seismic shift in this paradigm, democratising data access and transforming the very mechanisms through which human-machine interactions occur. This paper aims to delve into the intricate details of this transformative development, elaborating on the methodological advancements and practical implications of incorporating NLP into supply chain data analytics.

Linguistic Computational Models and Semantic Interpretation

At the core of NLP technologies lies advanced linguistic computational models capable of parsing, understanding, and generating human language. Utilizing machine learning algorithms along with linguistic rule-based methods, these models enable the semantic interpretation of user queries, thereby transcending the syntactic constraints traditionally associated with database languages. Techniques such as sentiment analysis, lexical semantics, and syntactic parsing are employed to accurately comprehend the nuanced meanings embedded within natural language queries.

Democratization of Data Access Through NLP

The advent of NLP serves to democratize the data access landscape significantly. Unlike conventional systems where proficiency in specialized database languages was a prerequisite, NLP technologies provide an egalitarian platform where personnel, irrespective of their technical expertise, can engage in data extraction and analysis. This widens the scope of user engagement with the database, opening up opportunities for cross-disciplinary insights and enriched decision-making.

Academic Discourse on NLP's Transformative Impact

An escalating body of scholarly literature has focused its lens on the transformative potential of NLP technologies, particularly within the realm of data analytics and supply chain management. Empirical studies and theoretical frameworks suggest that the translation of complex numerical and relational data into intuitive linguistic forms stands as a watershed moment in data analytics. These studies often employ a variety of methodologies, from case studies to computational simulations, to demonstrate the significant improvements in operational efficiency achieved through NLP integration.

Implications for Human-Machine Interaction and Decision-making

One of the most salient contributions of NLP technologies is the profound alteration in the quality and efficiency of human-machine interactions. By reducing the cognitive load associated with data querying and interpretation, NLP facilitates a more seamless, efficient, and expedited decision-making process. This has practical ramifications in various aspects of supply chain management, from inventory control to logistics optimization, by enabling quicker responses to real-time data and emerging situations.

In summary, the incorporation of Natural Language Processing technologies in supply chain data analytics heralds a pivotal advancement in the field. Through advanced computational models and semantic interpretation, NLP serves to democratize data access and engender more efficient and intuitive human-machine interfaces. The scholarly discourse substantiates these transformative effects, pointing to a future where NLP technologies will likely become indispensable tools in supply chain management and data analytics at large.

The Integration of Collaborative Robots (Cobots) in Contemporary Inventory Management: A Comprehensive Multidisciplinary Study on Efficiency and Workplace Safety Paradigms

The realm of modern industrial workplaces has been profoundly transformed by the inception of collaborative robots, commonly referenced as 'cobots.' These entities epitomise the zenith of technological advancement in fostering human-robot synergies in professional environments. Distinctively engineered to work in harmony with human counterparts rather than merely substituting them, cobots have become indispensable in undertaking a plethora of tasks. These tasks, which predominantly encompass repetitive or intrinsically hazardous attributes, span from meticulous sorting, dexterous lifting, to the precision-oriented placement of merchandise and an assortment of other critical operations.

To meticulously understand the multi-faceted implications of cobot integration, a plethora of industrial evaluations and erudite investigations have been undertaken. These comprehensive studies predominantly echo a recurrent theme: the assimilation of cobots within the intricate fabric of inventory management paradigms culminates in remarkable surges in operational productivity. Simultaneously, there is an impressive augmentation in adherence to established workplace safety protocols. This is palpably evidenced by the pronounced diminution in human exposure to perilous operational environments and a conspicuous decline in occurrences of repetitive stress maladies among the human workforce.

To encapsulate, the contemporary phase marked by the emergence of self-evolving supply chain systems, advanced Natural Language Processing (NLP) techniques for intricate data interpretation, and the strategic inclusion of cobots signifies a groundbreaking era in the annals of supply chain management. These avant-garde innovations not only accentuate the pivotal role of cutting-edge technology in bolstering operational prowess but also epitomise the harmonious interplay of machine learning, natural language processing, and robotics. This trinity effectively bolsters the resilience, flexibility, and overall adaptability of supply chain operations, heralding a promising future for the industry.

Quantum Computing for the Computational Advancement of Optimisation Problems in Inventory Management Systems

The advent of quantum computing is poised to usher in an era of unprecedented computational capabilities, heralding a paradigmatic shift in a plethora of sectors, from cryptography to material science. However, one area that is generating considerable scholarly intrigue is the application of quantum computing in the domain of inventory management. While quantum computing remains a nascent technology, its prospective influence on solving intricate optimisation challenges—especially those that classical computing platforms find computationally intractable or prohibitively time-consuming—has sparked significant academic discourse.

Computational Limitations of Classical Systems in Tackling Optimisation Problems

Classical computing paradigms, built upon von Neumann architecture, have historically been beset by limitations in effectively resolving complex optimisation conundrums. Examples of these vexing issues include but are not limited to, the Traveling Salesman Problem (TSP), Vehicle Routing Problems, and the optimisation of expansive, multi-objective, and multi-echelon supply chain networks. These challenges often entail NP-hard or NP-complete problems, where computational time increases exponentially with the growth in problem size, making them impractical to solve within reasonable time frames for large-scale systems.

The Quantum Computing Paradigm: A Transformative Approach to Optimisation

Quantum computing, grounded in the principles of quantum mechanics, holds the promise of solving certain categories of problems in polynomial time as opposed to the exponential time necessitated by classical counterparts. Leveraging quantum bits (qubits) over classical bits allows quantum algorithms to explore multiple solutions concurrently through superposition and entanglement, thus fundamentally altering the computational landscape for optimisation tasks.

Preliminary Scholarly Investigations into Quantum Algorithms and Optimisation Theory

Initial forays into the synthesis of quantum algorithms with optimisation theory have yielded intriguing results. Algorithms like Grover's and Shor's have already demonstrated quantum advantage for specific problem classes, and the development of quantum algorithms tailored for optimisation tasks, such as Quantum Approximate Optimization Algorithms (QAOA), suggests that once the technology matures, a quantum leap in computational capability is foreseeable.

Implications for Inventory Management

The maturation of quantum computing could precipitate a transformative impact on inventory management systems by enabling real-time optimisation of highly complex, dynamic systems. In turn, this would confer an unparalleled ability to significantly mitigate operational expenditures and enhance service levels. The net effect would be the establishment of a compelling competitive edge, particularly salient in the context of the increasingly labyrinthine and competitive global supply chain ecosystem.

Although quantum computing is still in its formative stages, the initial scholarly investigations underscore its prodigious potential to revolutionise the field of inventory management. By obviating the computational bottlenecks that currently stymie classical computing systems, quantum computing stands poised to offer radical improvements in solving complex optimisation problems, thereby heralding a new era in efficient, cost-effective, and agile inventory management in an increasingly intricate global landscape.

13. CONCLUSION: UNLOCKING EFFICIENCY THROUGH INVENTORY MANAGEMENT

Synthesis of Salient Concepts and Strategic Frameworks

In the ensuing discourse, we endeavour to encapsulate the quintessential principles and stratagems that have been meticulously elaborated upon throughout the volume. The objective of this summative exploration is to serve as an intellectual refresher for professionals situated in various echelons of the supply chain hierarchy—warehouse managers, inventory control specialists, and practitioners of supply chain management—with a particular emphasis on the nuances of inventory management. By revisiting and cogitating upon these axiomatic principles, practitioners are empowered with the intellectual arsenal necessary to optimize inventory systems, thereby augmenting the overarching efficiency of supply chain operations.

- **The Imperative of Optimal Inventory Levels:** Firstly, the book places a concentrated focus on the quintessential role of preserving an optimal level of inventory within a warehousing environment. The objective is to fine-tune the precarious equilibrium between overstocking and under-stocking, a balance critical to satisfying customer expectations while simultaneously attenuating operational expenditures. Employing an array of methodologies such as Economic Order Quantity (EOQ), Just-In-Time (JIT) Inventory Systems, and the computation of Safety Stock levels, provides a multifaceted framework through which inventory levels can be effectively modulated. Through the nuanced comprehension of these techniques, inventory managers are poised to curate a warehouse environment replete with optimal levels of stock, responsive to variances in both demand and supply.

- **Inventory Classification Paradigms:** A subsequent pivotal construct discussed in this work is the implementation of systematic inventory categorisation paradigms. This entails the stratification of inventory items in accordance with specific attributes, such as demand volatility and fiscal significance. Techniques such as ABC analysis, Pareto-based evaluations, and XYZ segmentation serve as the cornerstone methodologies for such classifications. By strategically allocating managerial focus and resources towards items of higher fiscal value and demand frequency, whilst concurrently optimising the management protocol for low-value, low-frequency items, organisations are better positioned to achieve operational alacrity, thereby reducing latent inefficiencies.

- **The Salience of Precise Demand Forecasting:** The book further delves into the seminal role played by accurate demand forecasting in the inventory management matrix. Utilising a confluence of historical data analytics, current market trends, and emerging demand patterns, warehouse managers are capacitated to make informed, empirically-grounded decisions pertaining to inventory accretion and depletion cycles. Accurate demand forecasting not only mitigates the risks associated with stock-outs and overstocking but also buttresses more effective long-term strategic planning.

- **Collaborative Synergies within the Supply Chain:** Additionally, the treatise explores the indispensability of fostering collaboration and seamless communication amongst the various nodes of the supply chain network. Cultivating robust relationships with suppliers, customers, and other vested stakeholders engenders an ecosystem conducive for efficacious inventory management. Through the assiduous sharing of information, the harmonisation of demand forecasting, and the actualisation of Collaborative Planning, Forecasting, and Replenishment (CPFR) models, practitioners can substantially ameliorate inventory visibility and truncate lead times, thereby enhancing operational responsiveness.

- **Technological Enablers of Inventory Optimisation:** Lastly, the manuscript underscores the transformative potential of technological implementations in the arena of inventory management. Advanced Warehouse Management Systems (WMS), Enterprise Resource Planning (ERP) suites, and analytical tools equipped with machine learning algorithms collectively offer real-time visibility into inventory metrics, facilitate automation of cumbersome manual processes, and generate actionable insights via data analytics. Leveraging these technologically-augmented functionalities allows inventory managers to not only streamline operational processes but also formulate decisions grounded in empirical evidence.

In summation, this subchapter serves as a holistic consolidation of the multifaceted principles and strategies germane to the realm of inventory management. By rigorously engaging with these foundational paradigms, practitioners across various segments of supply chain management are endowed with the intellectual scaffolding requisite for effectuating improvements in inventory regulation, operational cost reduction, and elevating customer satisfaction metrics. The practical application of these strategies culminates in a marked enhancement in the overall efficacy and robustness of supply chain operations.

The Imperative of Sustained Enhancement in Inventory Management: A Scholarly Perspective

In the exigent milieu of supply chain management, the notion of continuous improvement transcends mere terminological fad, establishing itself as an indispensable axiom critical to the viability and prosperity of any organisational entity. Those who serve in critical roles as Warehouse Managers, Inventory Managers, and Supply Chain Management Practitioners must rigorously comprehend the centrality of continuous improvement as it pertains to inventory management, thereby achieving a meticulous refinement of supply chain efficiency.

- **The Quintessential Role of Inventory Management in Organisational Success:** Inventory management constitutes an integral facet in the overarching architecture of business success. By guaranteeing the judicious availability of requisite products—aligned temporally, quantitatively, and geographically—efficient inventory management serves as the cornerstone for optimal operational efficacy. However, within the milieu of today's acutely competitive business landscape, the rudimentary practice of managing inventory lacks the requisite robustness to assure sustained competitive advantage. Ergo, an unrelenting commitment to improvement is not just commendable, but rather imperative, for remaining not only viable but also competitive in meeting contemporary consumer exigencies.

- **Diagnosing and Mitigating Operational Inefficiencies:** One of the paramount justifications for the endorsement of continuous improvement within the realm of inventory management lies in its efficacious capacity to unearth and eradicate operational inefficiencies. Through the perpetual assessment and reevaluation of existing processes, warehouse management can discern operational bottlenecks, truncate cycle times, and diminish material and temporal wastage. The subsequent outcomes are manifold: augmentation in productivity metrics, decrement in operational expenditures, and amplification in customer satisfaction indices. In sum, continuous improvement acts as a catalyst that streamlines operational modalities, thus facilitating a coherent and effective trajectory for inventory from the point of procurement through to distribution.

- **Adaptability in a Dynamic Business Ecosystem:** Moreover, in an era characterised by unrelenting technological advancements and rapidly oscillating market trends, organisational stasis serves as a recipe for obsolescence. Continuous improvement instils an indispensable degree of agility, rendering organisations sufficiently adaptable to evolving market vicissitudes. Through the assimilation of cutting-edge technologies, the espousal of industry best practices, and a commitment to remaining au courant with emergent trends and customer predilections, inventory managers can fine-tune their supply chain strategies and thereby secure a robust competitive footing.

- **Cultivating a Culture of Organisational Innovation:** Beyond operational benefits, the commitment to continuous improvement cultivates an organisational culture steeped in the principles of innovation. By incentivising the workforce to proactively offer ideas and recommendations, organisations can harness a reservoir of collective wisdom and experiential learning. Such an organisational culture not only boosts employee morale and a sense of ownership but also gives rise to disruptive solutions and process enhancements capable of revolutionising conventional paradigms of inventory management.

In summation, the principle of continuous improvement is not merely an optional initiative but an unequivocal necessity for professionals engaged in the specialised domain of inventory management. By continually pursuing avenues for enhancement and refinement, organisations are better positioned to diagnose and ameliorate inefficiencies, adapt to the flux inherent in market dynamics, and engender a culture of innovation. Thus, the conscientious adoption of continuous improvement serves as the linchpin for unlocking operational efficiency and optimising supply chain management, ensuring long-term organisational viability and competitiveness in an ever-volatile business environment.

A Scholarly Call to Action: Strategic Imperatives for Warehouse Managers and Inventory Practitioners in Modern Supply Chain Management

In the complex landscape of modern supply chain management, the role of warehouse managers and inventory practitioners is of pivotal importance. The efficacious handling of inventory serves as the linchpin for an organisation's overall supply chain efficacy, effectively acting as the fulcrum on which both upstream and downstream activities are balanced. This subchapter endeavours to articulate a comprehensive call to action for professionals responsible for inventory management, accentuating a suite of proactive measures designed to enhance operational performance, thereby engendering a cascade of benefits that permeate the entire supply chain.

- **Recognising the Imperative for Robust Inventory Management:** The first and most cardinal aspect that merits recognition is the indispensability of sound inventory management practices. A lack of precision in this domain can engender a myriad of operational hindrances, including but not limited to stock-outs, superfluous inventory levels, escalating carrying costs, and the subsequent erosion of customer satisfaction. By meticulously optimising inventory management protocols, professionals can not only mitigate these detrimental outcomes but also galvanize a series of positive reverberations, such as augmented customer satisfaction, cost-efficiency, and the overall streamlined functioning of the supply chain.

- **Technological Advancements: The Vanguard of Modern Inventory Management:** As we navigate the digital age, it becomes imperative for warehouse managers and inventory practitioners to embrace state-of-the-art inventory management technologies and methodologies. The deployment of sophisticated inventory management systems that offer real-time insights into inventory levels, fluctuating demand paradigms, and holistic supply chain performance can act as a force multiplier. By incorporating such systems, you do not merely streamline the transactional aspects of inventory management but imbue the decision-making process with empirical rigor, thereby enabling superior decisions relating to stock replenishment strategies, demand forecasting algorithms, and the intricacies of order fulfilment.

- **The Necessity for Inter-Organisational Collaboration:** In the era of interconnected supply networks, unilateral decision-making is suboptimal. Actively fostering robust partnerships with suppliers and customers is a non-negotiable requisite for achieving inventory management excellence. Through the bilateral sharing of forecast data, symbiotic engagement in demand planning exercises, and the exploration of innovative paradigms like Vendor-Managed Inventory (VMI) programs, inventory managers can unlock synergies that result in compressed lead times, minimised stock-outs, and optimised inventory levels across the supply network.

- **Continuous Improvement as an Operational Mantra:** The concept of perpetual improvement is woven into the fabric of superior inventory management. This necessitates the regular scrutiny of key performance indicators (KPIs) in the inventory domain, coupled with the implementation of best-in-class methodologies like Lean and Just-in-Time (JIT) inventory systems. These systems aim to systematically eradicate waste, minimize carrying costs, and enhance operational agility. Moreover, the introduction of automation and robotics into warehouse operations augments both the accuracy and the speed of inventory-related tasks, engendering a new echelon of operational efficiency.

- **Investing in Human Capital:** The Cornerstone of Sustainable Excellence: No technological or process innovation can supplant the need for a highly skilled and knowledgeable inventory management team. Therefore, investment in the professional growth of team members is not an option, but a strategic imperative. A commitment to ongoing training, the attainment of specialised certifications, and staying abreast of emerging industry trends will imbue your team with the competencies needed to instantiate best practices and foster an environment conducive to continuous improvement.

To encapsulate, the role of warehouse managers and inventory practitioners extends far beyond mere custodianship of goods; they serve as the architects of supply chain efficiency. By integrating cutting-edge technologies, catalysing collaboration with supply chain partners, inscribing a culture of continuous improvement, and diligently investing in the professional development of their teams, these professionals wield the power to not only optimize inventory management but to elevate the performance of the entire supply chain. Hence, taking action on these multifaceted fronts is not just advisable; it is an exigent mandate for any organisation aiming for supply chain excellence.

Appendix A: Glossary of Terms

The realm of inventory management and supply chain optimisation brims with specialised terms and acronyms. This comprehensive glossary aims to elucidate these terms, serving as a navigational compass for readers of "**Mastering the Chain: A Comprehensive Guide to Elevating Efficiency through Strategic Inventory Management.**"

A
ABC Analysis: A categorisation technique for inventory based on its importance in terms of value, volume, or turnover rate.
Artificial Intelligence (AI): Computational systems designed to simulate human cognitive processes, often deployed in tasks like demand forecasting and data analysis.

B
Barcode: A machine-readable data representation, widely used for inventory identification and tracking.
Blockchain: A secure, decentralised digital ledger technology employed for enhancing transparency and traceability in supply chains.

C
Collaborative Robots (Cobots): Robots intended to work in tandem with human operators, commonly used in warehousing for tasks such as sorting and picking.
Cycle Counting: A continual auditing method that involves counting a subset of inventory items regularly to ensure accuracy.

D
Demand Forecasting: The prediction of future demand using historical data and analytics, integral for accurate inventory planning.
Drone Technology: The utilization of unmanned aerial vehicles (UAVs) for diverse inventory management tasks including surveillance and auditing.

E
Economic Order Quantity (EOQ): A model that calculates the ideal order quantity to minimize total holding and ordering costs.
E-commerce: The conduct of commercial transactions over the internet, presenting unique inventory management challenges.

F
Fill Rate: A performance metric gauging the percentage of customer demand met through immediate stock availability.
Future Trends: Emerging developments and technologies likely to influence inventory management.

G
Gamification: The application of game elements in non-game contexts, commonly used for employee training and

motivation.
Global and Distributed Inventory Systems: Multi-location inventory systems that could span international territories.

H
Holding Costs: The costs of storing unsold inventory, encompassing elements like warehouse space, utilities, and insurance.

I
Inventory Accuracy: The extent to which the physical inventory matches the data recorded in inventory management systems.
Internet of Things (IoT): A network of physical objects embedded with sensors and software to collect and share data, used for real-time inventory monitoring.

J
Just-In-Time (JIT): An inventory management approach aimed at reducing in-process inventory and its associated costs.

K
Key Performance Indicators (KPIs): Metrics used to evaluate the effectiveness of operations and identify areas for improvement.
Kitting: The process of grouping, packaging, and supplying separate but related items as one unit.

L
Lead Time: The amount of time that elapses between placing an order and receiving it.
Lean Manufacturing: A systematic method for waste minimisation without sacrificing productivity.

M
Machine Learning: A subset of AI that allows systems to learn from data and improve their performance over time.
Multi-Channel Fulfilment: The practice of using multiple channels to fulfil customer orders.

N
Natural Language Processing (NLP): The use of algorithms to analyse human language, useful for data analytics in supply chains.
Network Optimisation: The strategic allocation of resources and activities across the supply chain network for optimal performance.

O
Omni-Channel Retailing: A retail strategy that integrates different shopping methods available to consumers, such as online and in-store.
Order Picking: The process of finding and extracting products from a warehouse to fulfil customer orders.

P
Perfect Order Performance: A metric that evaluates the effectiveness of the supply chain in delivering orders completely, on time, and in perfect condition.
Predictive Analytics: The use of statistics and modeling to determine future performance based on current and historical data.

Q
Quantum Computing: An emerging technology expected to vastly outperform classical computing, particularly in optimisation problems.
Quality Control: Procedures intended to ensure a product or service adheres to a defined set of quality criteria.

R
Reorder Point (ROP): The inventory level at which a new order should be placed to replenish stock before it runs out.
RFID (Radio-Frequency Identification): A technology used for automatic identification and data capture.

S
Safety Stock: Extra inventory kept on hand to mitigate the risks of stock-outs.
Supply Chain Collaboration: Strategic cooperation between various parties in a supply chain to achieve mutual business goals.

T
Trade-offs: Choices that involve losing one quality or aspect in return for gaining another.
Turnover Rate: The rate at which inventory is sold and replaced over a given time period.

U
Upstream and Downstream: Terms that refer to the stages before and after a particular point in the supply chain,

respectively.

V

Vendor Managed Inventory (VMI): An arrangement where the supplier takes on the responsibility for managing the inventory levels at the customer's storage facilities.

Voice-Directed Warehousing: The use of voice directions to guide warehouse employees in fulfilling tasks like picking, packing, and restocking.

W

Warehouse Management System (WMS): Software applications that support day-to-day operations in a warehouse.

Work-in-Process (WIP): Inventory that is currently being transformed into a finished good.

X

X-docking: A logistics strategy where products from a supplier or manufacturer are distributed directly to a customer or retail chain with minimal handling or storage time.

Appendix B: Regulatory Landscape

As supply chain and inventory management practices increasingly become a global endeavour, understanding the kaleidoscope of regulatory frameworks is no longer optional—it's a necessity. In this appendix, we delve into federal, state, and international regulations that may impact your supply chain operations, outlining essential compliance measures and risk mitigation strategies to ensure you're operating within legal boundaries.

Section 1: Federal Regulations

- **Federal Trade Commission (FTC)**
  Oversight of deceptive and unfair business practices.
  Compliance Requirements: Honest advertising, consumer privacy, and ethical business conduct.

- **Occupational Safety and Health Administration (OSHA)**
  Workplace safety in warehousing and distribution centers.
  Compliance Requirements: Safety guidelines, incident reports, worker protections.

- **U.S. Customs and Border Protection (CBP)**
  Import and export controls.
  Compliance Requirements: Customs documentation, duty payments, restrictions, and tariff classifications.

- **Federal Maritime Commission (FMC)**
  Regulations affecting shipping by sea.
  Compliance Requirements: Licensing, financial responsibility, and trade practices.

Section 2: State-Specific Regulations

- **Sales Tax**
  Applicable to transactions that occur within state lines.
  Compliance Requirements: Collection, reporting, and remittance of state-specific sales tax.

- **State Environmental Protection Agencies**
  Oversight on waste management and emissions.
  Compliance Requirements: Permits, waste disposal methods, and sustainability practices.

- **State Labor Laws**
  Rules around employee welfare, benefits, and rights.
  Compliance Requirements: Minimum wage, worker's compensation, and employee benefits.

Section 3: International Regulations

- **European Union's General Data Protection Regulation (GDPR)**
  Data protection and privacy.
  Compliance Requirements: Data handling, user consent, and data protection measures.

- **World Customs Organization (WCO)**
  Harmonized System Codes for global trading.
  Compliance Requirements: Correct product coding for customs declaration.

- **International Chamber of Commerce (ICC)**
  Incoterms for international trade.
  Compliance Requirements: Delivery terms, risks, and costs.

Section 4: Compliance and Risk Mitigation Strategies

- **Regular Audits**
  Conduct periodic internal and external audits to assess compliance with federal, state, and international laws.

- **Documentation**
  Ensure meticulous record-keeping for potential audits or legal actions.

- **Employee Training**
  Educate your staff on the importance of compliance and the practical steps they need to take.

- **Legal Consultation**
  Consult with legal experts specialized in federal, state, and international trade laws to confirm you are on secure legal ground.

- **Technology Solutions**
  Leverage compliance software and technologies to aid in monitoring, reporting, and adhering to regulations.

Embarking on a journey through the labyrinthine world of regulations may seem daunting, but consider this appendix as your compass—designed to navigate through the complexities of laws and guidelines that affect your inventory and supply chain operations. Be it federal, state, or international waters you tread, the mantra remains the same: stay compliant, stay ahead.

Appendix C: Inventory Management Checklist

As the adage goes, what gets measured gets managed. In the dynamic realm of inventory management, vigilance and strategic planning are key to maintaining a well-oiled supply chain. This checklist serves as a comprehensive toolkit for businesses striving for efficiency and operational excellence in inventory management. Use it as a yardstick to measure your existing operations and as a roadmap for continuous improvement.

Regular Monitoring and Strategic Adjustments:

Initial Inventory Audit
Ensure an initial complete count of all existing inventory.
Verify that physical counts align with recorded data in your management system.
Identify discrepancies and determine root causes.

Ongoing Cycle Counts
Schedule regular cycle counts, either random sampling or full counts depending on the size and complexity of the inventory.
Utilize barcode or RFID systems for accurate and quick counts.

Demand Forecasting
Update demand forecasts periodically to reflect actual sales data, market trends, and other external variables like seasonality.
Validate your forecasting model's predictions with actual outcomes.

Safety Stock Assessment
Regularly review safety stock levels to ensure optimal amounts that mitigate stockout risks but also minimize carrying costs.
Take lead times into account for every SKU.

Supplier Performance Review
Assess supplier performance in terms of reliability, quality, and timeliness.
Re-negotiate contracts or seek alternative suppliers if performance metrics are consistently subpar.

Cost-Benefit Analysis
Conduct a full cost-benefit analysis focusing on ordering, carrying, and stockout costs.

Explore bulk purchase discounts, and balance them against the cost of holding extra inventory.

Technology Assessment
Keep your software up-to-date and scout for new technologies that can provide competitive advantages.
Review technology requirements annually and budget for necessary upgrades or transitions.

Employee Skill Audit and Training
Perform skills audits to identify areas where staff training may improve efficiency or reduce error.
Invest in training programs, both for new employees and for ongoing development.

Waste Identification and Minimization
Track and identify any form of waste including obsolete inventory, damaged goods, or inefficient processes.
Implement strategies to minimize waste, such as Just-in-Time (JIT) methods or donation of obsolete items.

Customer Feedback Loop
Implement mechanisms to collect customer feedback on order accuracy, delivery speed, and product quality.
Address issues proactively and adjust inventory strategies accordingly.

KPI Monitoring
Use real-time dashboards to track Key Performance Indicators (KPIs) like inventory turnover, fill rate, and carrying costs.
Re-calibrate your business strategies based on these metrics.

Regulatory Compliance Checks
Regularly review operations to ensure compliance with industry standards and regulations, such as OSHA for warehousing safety or FDA for food and drug storage.
Maintain records for compliance audits and inspections.

Continuous Improvement Culture
Encourage a culture of continuous improvement where employees are motivated to identify and solve inefficiencies.
Consider implementing a rewards system for suggestions that lead to measurable improvements.

Quarterly Strategy Review
Conduct a comprehensive quarterly review of your inventory management strategy, bringing together cross-functional teams for a holistic analysis.

Annual Benchmarking
Annually, compare your performance metrics with industry benchmarks to identify areas for improvement or investment.

This checklist is not a one-size-fits-all solution but a guide to be tailored to the unique needs and complexities of your business. By adhering to these steps, you're well on your way to mastering the chain and elevating efficiency through strategic inventory management.

Appendix F: Typologies of Inventory: A Comprehensive Categorization

The inventory management paradigm varies considerably across different business sectors. As such, delineating the categorial types of inventories is an exigent task for practitioners seeking to optimize the inventory management process. This appendix aims to elucidate the prevalent types of inventories encountered in various business settings.

Types of Inventories

- **Raw Materials:** Fundamentally, these are the elemental substances utilized in the production pipeline. The procurement, storage, and management of raw materials are essential for initiating the manufacturing process.

- **Work-in-Progress (WIP):** These inventories constitute unfinished goods residing in various stages of the production workflow. Managing WIP inventory is critical for just-in-time production schedules and operational efficiency.

- **Finished Goods:** This category encompasses manufactured products that are wholly completed and are in a sale-ready condition. Effective management of finished goods inventory correlates directly with customer satisfaction metrics and revenue realization.

- **MRO (Maintenance, Repair, and Operations) Inventory:** These are quintessential items that facilitate the upkeep, repair, and the efficient operation of business processes but are not directly involved in production.

- **Pipeline Inventory:** Denotes goods that are in the transitive phase between different geographic locations or stages of production. Managing pipeline inventory efficiently can result in cost savings and improved supply chain agility.

- **Perishable Goods:** These are inventory items characterized by their limited temporal shelf-life. The storage, rotation, and logistical handling of perishable goods require meticulous planning to minimize spoilage and waste.

- **Consignment Inventory:** These are commodities that are housed by a retailer but remain the property of the supplier until they are sold. The complexities of consignment inventory often involve legal contractual obligations and financial risk sharing.

- **Cyclical Inventory:** This refers to inventory surplus that is strategically amassed to counteract seasonal or cyclical fluctuations in demand. Mastering cyclical inventory levels can act as a hedge against market volatility.

Appendix G: Styles of Inventory Management: A Scholarly Exploration

Inventory management is not a monolithic endeavour but a nuanced practice that is contingent upon a range of variables including business type, volume of goods, and supply chain complexity. This appendix aims to provide a scholarly overview of the diverse styles of inventory management prevalent in contemporary business.

Inventory Management Styles

- **Just-in-Time (JIT):** This methodology pivots on the principle of minimalism, retaining only indispensable items requisite for immediate production needs. Originating from Japanese manufacturing practices, JIT is renowned for its efficiency but requires precise coordination and robust supplier relationships.
- **Bulk Shipments:** Predominantly applicable for items with extended shelf lives, this style involves the acquisition and warehousing of commodities in large quantities. Economies of scale are often achievable but are counterbalanced by elevated carrying costs and potential obsolescence.
- **ABC Analysis:** This analytical framework involves the segregation of inventory into three hierarchical categories—A, B, and C—based on their financial or operational significance. Category A items are generally high-value, whereas C items are low-value. This stratification assists in targeted inventory optimization strategies.
- **Dropshipping:** In this modality, the retailer acts as an intermediary, facilitating the direct transfer of goods from the manufacturer to the end-consumer. This eliminates the need for inventory holding by the retailer but often involves complex logistics and quality control issues.
- **Cross-docking:** This logistic strategy involves the immediate transfer of inbound goods to outbound transportation with minimal warehousing time. While reducing inventory holding costs, it demands an agile and highly coordinated logistical infrastructure.

Appendix H: Comprehensive Analysis of Inventory Management Approaches, Evaluative Checklists, and Auditory Techniques in the Realm of E-Commerce

The ascendancy of e-commerce as a commercial modality has engendered a seismic shift in how inventory management is conceptualised and executed. Given its centrality in shaping both operational efficiency and customer engagement, inventory management in e-commerce settings requires multifaceted and nuanced strategies. This appendix seeks to expound on variegated styles of inventory management bespoke to e-commerce, while concurrently providing detailed evaluative checklists and auditory methodologies. This serves as a rigorous academic resource aimed at illuminating the labyrinthine aspects of inventory management in e-commerce for scholars, industry experts, and practitioners.

Typological Exegesis of Inventory Management Styles Customised for E-Commerce

- **Real-Time Demand-Driven Management:** This progressive style leverages immediate analytics and agile reordering protocols. Especially relevant for e-commerce ecosystems subject to capricious consumer demand patterns, this method dynamically adjusts inventory based on real-time data analytics, essentially functioning as an adaptive system to counter overstocking and under-stocking predicaments.

- **Omni-channel Inventory Unification:** Here, the principal objective is to achieve inventory harmonisation across various sales and distribution platforms—be it the primary e-commerce portal, affiliated digital marketplaces, or even physical storefronts, thereby transcending the traditional dichotomy between online and offline retail paradigms.

- **Deferred Delivery or Backordering:** Unlike conventional inventory models, this approach is predicated upon the consumer's proclivity for delayed gratification. It offers the advantage of optimising storage space while reducing holding costs, as purchase commitments are made in anticipation of future inventory.

- **Batch Prioritisation and Expiry Management:** Particularly salient for perishable goods or items with a finite usability timeframe, this strategy emphasises FIFO (First-In, First-Out) compliance, thus mitigating wastage and ensuring quality deliverance to the customer.

- **Automated Intelligence-Driven Reordering:** Incorporating machine learning algorithms and historical data analytics, this style minimizes human intervention by initiating automated reorders based on pre-defined stock level thresholds and seasonality factors.

Evaluative Checklist for Inventory Management in the E-Commerce Domain

- **Regularised Inventory Inspection:** Periodic audits for maintaining optimal SKU-specific stock levels, incorporating both high-frequency and slow-moving items.

- Metadata Quality Assurance: Consistent verification and updating of product descriptions, specifications, and SKU identifiers, to facilitate accurate and informed consumer purchasing decisions.

- **Strategic Supplier Relationships:** Establishment of a collaborative interface with suppliers, which includes real-time tracking of order statuses and ongoing assessments of contractual obligations.

- **Order Fulfilment Integrity:** Rigorous processes to ensure precise order preparation, inclusive of picking, packaging, and shipping, and to manage returns and cancellations efficiently.

- **Software and System Health Assessments:** A recurring evaluation of the technical robustness and functional efficacy of integrated software solutions, including their scalability and interoperability.

- **Statutory and Regulatory Compliance:** Ongoing diligence to ensure adherence to international trade regulations, including but not limited to customs duties, import/export restrictions, and consumer rights policies.

- **Temporal Demand Fluctuation Planning:** The incorporation of predictive analytics and machine learning models to pre-emptively manage inventory in alignment with forecasted demand variations, often related to seasonal events, sales promotions, or market trends.

Auditory Strategies for Inventory Management: Scholarly Guidelines

- **Scheduled Quantitative Audits:** Conducted either monthly or quarterly, these structured audits encapsulate a comprehensive review of inventory, segmented by various categories or product lines.

- **Randomized Spot-Check Analysis:** An unscheduled approach targeting specific, high-value or high-turnover items, thereby offering a snapshot of inventory health in a more agile but less comprehensive manner.

- **Rotational Cycle Counting:** A strategic technique that involves segmenting inventory into different subsets, which are then audited on a staggered schedule, providing a continuous yet focused evaluation of stock levels.

- **Annual Full-Scale Inventory Audit:** A comprehensive audit that includes the counting of every item in inventory, generally conducted annually to provide a holistic view and to serve as a point of calibration for other audit methods.

- **Documentary Cross-Verification:** Involves a stringent scrutiny of all transactional documents related to inventory—purchase orders, shipping manifests, and sales invoices—to authenticate or correct existing inventory records.

- **Digital System Audits:** A higher-order audit that assesses the reliability, security, and efficiency of automated inventory management systems, ensuring the accuracy of algorithmic calculations and the integrity of data storage and retrieval mechanisms.

www.ingramcontent.com/pod-product-compliance
Lightning Source LLC
LaVergne TN
LVHW070532070526
838199LV00075B/6761